D0800083

HISTORIC BUILDING FAÇADES

HISTORIC BUILDING FAÇADES

The Manual for Maintenance and Rehabilitation

NEW YORK LANDMARKS CONSERVANCY

William G. Foulks, *Editor*

PRESERVATION PRESS

JOHN WILEY & SONS, INC.

NEW YORK / CHICHESTER / WEINHEIM / BRISBANE / SINGAPORE / TORONTO

This text is printed on acid-free paper.

Copyright© 1997 by John Wiley & Sons, Inc.

All rights reserved. Published simultaneously in Canada.

Reproduction or translation of any part of this work beyond that permitted by Section 107 or 108 of the 1976 United States Copyright Act without the permission of the copyright owner is unlawful. Requests for permission or further information should be addressed to the Permissions Department, John Wiley & Sons, Inc., 605 Third Avenue, New York, NY 10158-0012.

This publication is designed to provide accurate and authoritative information in regard to the subject matter covered. It is sold with the understanding that the publisher is not engaged in rendering legal, accounting, or other professional services. If legal advise or other expert assistance is required, the services of a competent professional person should be sought.

The New York Landmarks Conservancy, founded in 1973, is a not-for-profit preservation organization that works in cooperation with public agencies, nonprofit organizations, and private developers to serve as a bridge between New York State's past and its future by preserving and revitalizing buildings and communities throughout the city and state. The Conservancy's technical assistance, publications and education programs, and grants and loans enable property owners to save buildings from disuse and neglect, stimulating community pride and renewal.

Library of Congress Cataloging in Publication Data:
Historic building façades: the manual for maintenance & rehabilition / the New York Landmarks Conservancy.
    p. cm.
   ISBN 0-471-14415-0 (pbk. : alk. paper)
    1. Exterior walls—Maintenance and repair. 2. Façades—Conservation and restoration. 3. Historic buildings—Conservation and restoration. I. New York Landmarks Conservancy.
TH2235.H56   1997
690'.2—dc20   96-36643
                                 CIP

Printed in the United States of America

10 9 8 7 6 5 4

CONTENTS

ON UNDERSTANDING THE HISTORIC FAÇADE

THROUGHOUT WESTERN HISTORY, until the recent past, the façade's significance stemmed from its origins as the exterior face a house and home presented to the world. It had been not merely a respectable feature of a building but actually its most important external surface—literally, the face the owner turned to the world. This façade discharged a number of functions simultaneously. Aside from the obvious task of weather protection, it was also the point of access and exit, as well as the main, if not the only, wall with daylight and outlook. These purely functional aspects made the window and front door its dominant feature. But the façade had another, and more portentous function: it served as an encoded statement of the owner's image—its wealth and status and artistic literacy. This would have been true for any building, of any pretensions—urban or rural, town house or plantation. But the façade became critically important in the town house, especially in American cities, where the ubiquitous gridiron system of street layout produced lots with narrow frontages. Only the street intersections yielded corner lots with more than one frontage open to daylight, outlook, and public access. Under such circumstances, the façade achieved an enormous strategic importance in communicating to the public world the owner's wealth, taste, and up-to-dateness.

This elaboration of the street façade for purely ideological polemics has a long and honorable history—stretching back to medieval times in Europe. In the reconstruction of war-ravished Old Town in Warsaw, Polish preservation architects were astonished to find that the burghers had repeatedly put new plaster façades on their old masonry town houses. Each façade had been remodeled in the then current vogue—Renaissance, Baroque, Rococo—some of them as close together as 60–70 years! This elaboration of the entrance façade as a critically important means of communicating the status of the householder, has continued down into the present day, at least in the domain of popular culture, in the form of the picture window and the 2- or 3-car garage.

But recently the elaboration of the façade purely for purposes of display has become discredited. In more sophisticated circles because of its connotations of artificiality, two-dimensionality, and vulgar display, it became regarded as a mask, which concealed not merely vanity but even dishonesty and mendacity.

Modernism in architecture, with its ethos of good form as deriving only from function strictly observed, is, of course, at the base of this moral take of position, which is now basic to most esthetic judgements. In the light of contemporary experience it is difficult to fault this new attitude toward the façade. However, today's preservationist should not allow himself to follow such modern attitudes when confronted with the task of preserving/restoring the esthetic integrity of America's historic façades. Seen in light of the ethos of the periods that created them, the traditional façade is an absolutely critical element. And contemporary anti-façadist attitudes must not be permitted to pollute their restoration.

To what extent the historic façade is to be manipulated today by the preservationist/restorationist depends upon the individual project. Unless the façade has been so mutilated by repeated interventions (remodeling) as to render its original logic unintelligible, it may be appropriate merely to curate it—i.e., preserve it in the state in which the curator has received it. But, if as is often the case, the client may want it to be restored to a certain date because of its own historical associations, then it may be necessary to return it to the visual condition of that specific period (i.e, removing later additions or modifications or restoring historic features lost in that process.) That decision must rest in the hands of its curators, who might want to follow the standard rules of the game.

And, here, the Landmarks Conservancy has set forth those standard rules of façade care as a part of a practical process of building stewardship and maintenance. When a building's caretaker understands façade materials and their conditions, as *Historic Building Façades* stresses is the critical first step, only then it is possible to formulate an appropriate remedy. I commend this book to all who care for the face that a historic building presents to the world: its façade.

JAMES MARSTON FITCH
Hon. AIA, Hon. FRIBA

PREFACE

RESEARCH AND PREPARATION of the original edition of this manual began as a response to a problem, first perceived as local but soon afterward understood to be national in scope. In May of 1979, a pedestrian in Manhattan was struck and killed by a piece of masonry that dislodged from a building façade and fell to the sidewalk. Nine months later, Local Law 10 (1980) "requiring periodic inspection of exterior walls and appurtenances of buildings" was enacted. As complying owners began to have their buildings inspected and repaired, preservationists became aware that the law was having adverse consequences; many ornamental projections such as cornices, balconies, lintels, and gargoyles were being removed to reduce the risk of future failures. Projections that often defined the character of otherwise monotonous building façades and contributed to the textures of the city's neighborhoods were being inadvertently victimized as a result of the law.

A survey of other cities showed that Local Law 10 was not an isolated response to the problem. Following a similar death, Chicago had revised its code in 1978 to include a requirement for critical examination of building façades and enclosures. Other cities followed with similar laws.

The New York Landmarks Conservancy, a private, not-for-profit organization committed to the preservation of New York's architectural heritage, was one of a number of civic groups concerned about the implementation of Local Law 10. While fully supporting the intent of the law to promote sound maintenance, the Conservancy attributed the removal of ornamental projections to, among other reasons, a lack of information concerning the construction and inspection of façades built with materials and details no longer used in standard practice. In 1983, the Conservancy commenced studying the use, deterioration, inspection, and rehabilitation of once commonly-employed building materials and components found in multistory urban structures with the intention of developing a manual for use by building owners, architects and engineers inspecting façades, public administrators reviewing their reports, and contractors correcting unsafe conditions, who seek to retain ornamental projections.

Historic Building Façades presents an approach to analyzing problems of and prescribing solutions for the façades of old buildings for building owners and professionals who have limited experience working with historic buildings. It shows how to discover what is wrong before proposing remedies. It also points out failures of many common solutions and provides guidelines for evaluating proposed solutions. The manual is not concerned exclusively with landmark buildings, which are protected against indiscriminate stripping and repair, but with all buildings that affect the appearance of historic urban communities.

ACKNOWLEDGMENTS

THIS REVISED EDITION of *Historic Building Façades* was made possible by grants from the Samuel H. Kress Foundation, the New York State Council on the Arts, and Brisk Waterproofing Company. Support for the first edition of the book was provided by the Design Arts Program of the National Endowment for the Arts, the National Heritage Trust (a program administered by the New York State Office of Parks, Recreation and Historic Preservation), and The J.M. Kaplan Fund.

The New York Landmarks Conservancy preserves and reuses architecturally significant buildings by providing grants, low-interest loans, and building conservation services. In communities throughout the City and State of New York, the Conservancy works with property owners to ensure the maintenance, repair, and restoration of homes, businesses, houses of worship, social service centers, cultural institutions, and buildings that serve a variety of other functions. The Conservancy is also a strong advocate for historic preservation issues, presents practical information through workshops and technical publications, and promotes the importance of preservation through lectures, tours, award programs, and other public events.

The Conservancy is grateful to the following professionals who served as advisors to the original study: Simon Breines, Jan C.K. Anderson, Cornelius F. Dennis, Leo Henrichs, Philip K. Howard, Michael Lynch, Frank Sanchis, Robert Silman, and Deborah Beck.

The original manual was developed from a study report prepared in 1983 and 1984. Some chapters of the original manual was prepared by the firm of Robert E. Meadows, P.C. Architect (Robert E. Meadows. Principal; William G. Foulks, Project Director; Dean K. Koga and Ulana Zakalak, Associates; Tracy Coffing, Gordon Loader, Zach Watson Rice). Other chapters were prepared by the firm of Liebman Ellis Melting, Architects and Planners (John Ellis, Principal; Gregory Dreicer, Consultant). The study was directed by the Technical Preservation Services center of the New York Landmarks Conservancy (Wesley Haynes, Manager; Mark Weber, Assistant Manager; Jane Jansen Seymour, Publications and Workshops Program

Coordinator; Elizabeth Igleheart, Research Assistant; Karen Patteson, Graphics Consultant; and Jean A. Kunkel, Director of Development).

The following people contributed to the effort behind assembling this book:

Mark A. Weber is director of the Technical Services Center at the New York Landmarks Conservancy. He is a preservationist and building conservator who oversees the Conservancy's program that provides technical assistance to the owners and stewards of New York's architecturally significant buildings and neighborhoods. Mr. Weber coordinated the revision and reorganization of the current edition of *Historic Building Façades*.

The staff of the New York Landmarks Conservancy who contributed to this book were Roger P. Lang, the director of Community Programs and Services, Ken M. Lustbader, the director of the Sacred Sites Program, and James V. Banta, technical program assistant for the Conservancy's Technical Services Center.

CONTRIBUTORS

William G. Foulks is an associate with John G. Waite Associates, Architects, PLLC. He has taught in the Program in Historic Preservation at Columbia University and for the past seventeen years has worked with architectural firms specializing in the restoration of significant historic buildings. Mr. Foulks edited and expanded the current edition of *Historic Building Façades*.

Frances Gale is training coordinator for the National Center for Preservation Technology and Training, in Natchitoches, Louisiana. She has a Master of Science in Historic Preservation from Columbia University and fifteen years of experience in the restoration of historic buildings and monuments. She is the author of several technical articles on masonry preservation, and lectures widely to architects, engineers, and contractors on conservation issues. Ms. Gale is a co-author of the sections pertaining to masonry cleaning.

Diane S. Kaese, AIA, is a senior architect with the Princeton, New Jersey, office of Wiss, Janney, Elstner Associates, Inc. She specializes in the evaluation, maintenance, and repair of buildings and building materials. Ms. Kaese is the author of the Concrete chapter.

Stephen J. Kelley, AIA, SE, is with the Chicago office of Wiss, Janney, Elstner Associates, Inc. He is involved in preservation technology, and he chairs the American Society for Testing and Materials (ASTM) Subcommittee on Building Preservation. Mr. Kelley was editor of the ASTM publication *Standards for Preservation and Rehabilitation* and is a co-author of the section pertaining to abrasive stone cleaning.

John Leeke is a well-recognized preservation consultant and craftsman based in Portland, Maine. He has been preserving historic buildings for 25 years and is the author of a technical publication series that advocates conservation planning and maintenance programming. Mr. Leeke is a contributing author of the Wood chapter.

Robert E. Meadows is the principal author and illustrator for the first edition of *Historic Building Façades*. After long service as a preservation architect based in New York City, he is now the Campus Architect for the University of Indiana.

Michael J. Scheffler is a consultant with the Chicago office of Wiss, Janney, Elstner Associates, Inc. He is a professional engineer specializing in the investigation and repair of building façades and curtain walls, particularly with regard to thin-stone veneers and sealants. Mr. Scheffler is a co-author of the Caulks and Sealants chapter.

Deborah Slaton is a senior architectural conservator with the Chicago office of Wiss, Janney, Elstner Associates, Inc., specializing in the investigation and conservation of construction materials. She is also a certified construction specifier. Ms. Slaton is a co-author of the Caulks and Sealants chapter.

John G. Waite, FAIA, is a principal of John G. Waite Associates, Architects, PLLC of Albany, New York, a nationally recognized practice that has been responsible for the restoration of many of America's most significant buildings. The author of more than fifty books and articles on historic preservation and building conservation, he was awarded the Harley J. McKee Award for Outstanding Contribution to the Field of Preservation Technology in 1995 by the Association for Preservation Technology. Mr. Waite is the author of the Cast Iron and Sheet Metal chapters.

Martin E. Weaver is a leading international specialist in the conservation of historic buildings and sites. He has a conservation consultant practice based in Nepean, Ontario, Canada, and in New York City. He is a professor in the Historic Preservation Program and director of the Center for Preservation Research at Columbia University. A prolific writer and lecturer, Weaver is the author of the standard textbook, *Conserving Buildings: A Guide to Techniques and Materials*, published by John Wiley & Sons, Inc. and the Preservation Press. Mr. Weaver is a contributing author of the Wood chapter.

George Segan Wheeler is Research Chemist in the Sherman Fairchild Center for Objects Conservation at the Metropolitan Museum of Art. His primary research interest is the study of consolidants for stone. Mr. Wheeler is the principal author of the Stone chapter.

INTRODUCTION

THE NATURE OF WALLS

AS ELEMENTS GIVING a building form, walls define a structure's limits and endow it with a visual presence. The forms of the walls and the qualities of the materials of which they are made—their shapes, colors, textures and detailing—define the character of a building and provide the basis for the image people have of it. The walls give a building scale, relating it to the people, the landscape, and the buildings around it. They also determine whether the building will be seen as a reference to the past or to the future. In addition to creating images, however, walls are important building systems with numerous functional purposes. In many cases, they support the rest of the building. In almost all cases, they form an envelope that protects the interior of the building and its inhabitants from abuses of water, air, sun, and other environmental forces. (Fig. I.1)

Walls built soundly enough to support themselves and related portions of the building could stand forever if no outside forces acted on them. But in reality, numerous external agents affect walls. The force of gravity pulls them down. Wind blows on them. Snow and ice piling up on roofs may put unanticipated loads on them. People also do unexpected things to them: they load them, cover them with coatings and emulsions, and even drive cars into them. Heat and cold cause walls to swell and shrink daily and, more significantly, with the seasons. Water freezes and thaws in walls, exerting pressure in the pores of materials forming them. Rain- and water-borne atmospheric pollutants dissolve and wear away both the wall's skin and its body. In addition, dirt in the air works inexorably toward making all walls the same color—a uniform, stable black.

Unfortunately, many people charged with the maintenance and repair of building façades become so preoccupied with the deterioration of walls and their components and the resulting problems and expense of repairs that they forget the many positive ways that walls contribute to our existence—both as individuals and as a society. Because

1

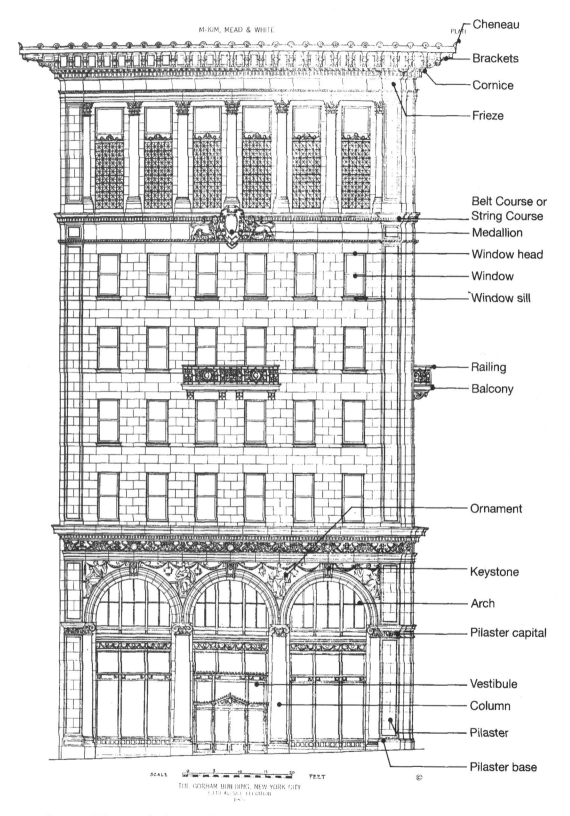

McKIM, MEAD & WHITE

Cheneau

Brackets

Cornice

Frieze

Belt Course or
String Course

Medallion

Window head

Window

Window sill

Railing

Balcony

Ornament

Keystone

Arch

Pilaster capital

Vestibule

Column

Pilaster

Pilaster base

SCALE 0 5 10 15 20 FEET

THE GORHAM BUILDING, NEW YORK CITY
FIFTH AVENUE ELEVATION

FIGURE I.1. *Façade showing the importance of decorative elements in defining a building's scale.*

these positive aspects of walls—the forms and presence they give to buildings, the scale they give to the street and to the neighborhood, and the historical references they provide—are as important as the negative, this study places as much emphasis on retaining a wall's appearance as it does on preserving or reestablishing its structural integrity and continuity.

If deterioration and decay were the only considerations, the ideal wall would be a plain, homogeneous, vertical surface—without joints, openings, or projections—made of a material unaffected by thermal expansion and contraction or by water or water vapor. But ideal walls do not exist. Materials are affected by changes in temperature and by contact with water. Joints separate units of like and different materials. Openings are usually required for access and to admit light and air. Walls often have projections both for functional and aesthetic reasons. The introduction of such openings and the use of projections immediately increases the potential for walls to deteriorate. (Fig. I.2)

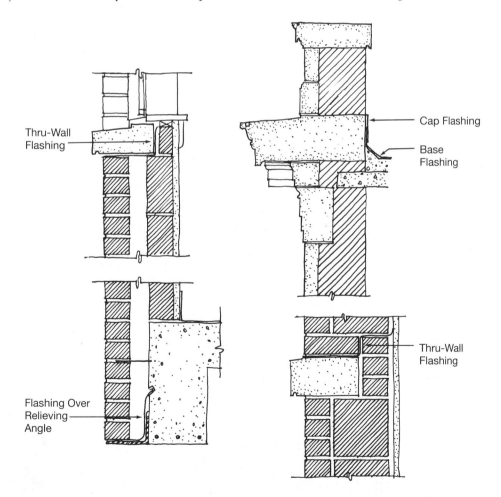

FIGURE I.2. *Different types of façade projections used for functional and aesthetic reasons increase the potential for water infiltration and subsequent building deterioration. Proper flashing at projections can minimize this problem.*

WALL ELEMENTS

Joints

Walls constructed of the building materials commonly used in the 19th and first half of the 20th centuries—stone, brick, terra-cotta, cast stone, cast iron, concrete, and wood—have many joints, or junctions, between units of material. There may be joints between units of the same material, such as between bricks or blocks of stone, and there may be joints between two different materials, such as between a masonry façade and window frames set into it. While all joints on the building surface must help to protect the materials of the façade and the interior of the building from damage by water and other exterior forces, different kinds of joints have different functions.

Joints between masonry units (such as those between bricks, blocks of stone, or between brick and stone) are of two basic types. In traditional masonry bearing wall construction—common throughout the 19th century and the early decades of the 20th century, and still common for small structures—the joints are part of the wall's structural system. These joints must act as an adhesive to glue the units, and, if the wall is to function properly, must take as much tensile, compressive, and shear stress as the masonry units themselves. The material in these joints—mortar, for example—must have physical characteristics compatible with those of the joined units together so that expansion, contraction, and the passage of water vapor will not affect them differently.

In curtain wall construction—a form of construction developed in the late 19th century and used in many buildings early in the 20th century and in all tall structures built in recent years—the exterior masonry skin is supported on a structural frame of iron, steel, or reinforced concrete. Some of the joints in the exterior skin on this type of façade are not structural or load-bearing. Such joints occur at connections between materials or between units of material supported independently. They allow for varying rates of expansion and contraction and water vapor permeability in different materials, and for release of the significant stresses that can build up in wide expanses of the same material. These joints must be filled with a material that remains flexible so that it can expand and contract in response to movements in the materials around it. In large expanses of wall, major mechanical expansion joints may be installed to allow for even more movement than is possible in joints filled with a flexible material.

Joints between different materials—such as those between the glass in a window and the wood or metal frame and those between the window frame and the masonry wall—traditionally have been, and still are, filled with a flexible material to allow for varying rates of expansion and contraction and water vapor permeability in different materials.

Joint failure in the façade may allow water to enter, which can cause further damage to the joints and to the materials of the wall. Initial problems usually are cosmetic, but further deterioration may lead to failure of the materials and to failure of the structure itself.

Openings

Walls usually have openings—windows and doors—to admit light and air and to permit entrance and egress. As essential as they are, however, openings in walls pose potential problems. At the most basic level, the member across the top of the opening, or lintel, must support the portion of the wall above it; if the lintel fails, either from improper design or from deterioration, a portion of the wall will sag and may eventually collapse. Openings also provide several locations through which water can seep behind the wall's surface. Unless window openings are carefully designed, water running down the façade, for example, may run back under the window lintel or under the window sill, or enter through the sill if, as in many older buildings, the sill has joints that have not been maintained. Joints between the surface material of the wall and the frame of the window must also be properly constructed and maintained to exclude water. The window material itself, most often wood in old buildings, must be protected. If it is not, water entering it may damage not only the window members but the surrounding wall as well.

Projections

Projections from the plane of a wall serve many aesthetic functions, such as providing a strong cap to a building's design, emphasizing openings, and creating scale and visual interest by breaking up the façade plane. They also can help to prevent water from reaching the wall surface and openings. Unfortunately, they also can be sources of trouble. The many elements that project from building façades for functional and aesthetic reasons include pediments, cornices, stringcourses, sills, lintels, balconies, and other ornaments. Water and snow accumulating on the tops of such projections can enter any cracked or open joints in the wall above these elements. Water can also run back along the undersides of projecting horizontal surfaces and enter openings in the joints below. If the projecting element itself has joints that are not properly maintained, water can enter and deteriorate the element and any interior supporting structure. As soon as water enters, the process of deterioration begins.

The structural support system for projecting elements is especially important since, unlike elements within the plane of the wall, projecting elements exert a twisting or rotational force around the point of support. If this force is not properly resisted, it may lead to deflections—stressing other façade members—or to failure. If, because of any of these or other situations, deterioration of a wall begins, these projecting elements pose a more serious hazard than do nonprojecting façade elements. Loose pieces within the plane of the wall may remain even if joints or supports give way because gravity pulls them down on the pieces below them. A projecting element whose supports have corroded or otherwise deteriorated will often be pulled down by gravity—falling to the ground below and potentially harming people or property in its path. (Fig. I.3)

One common element that projects from a building wall, although vertically rather

FIGURE I.3. *The failure of projecting façade elements presents a hazard to people and property below.* James V. Banta, New York Landmarks Conservancy

than horizontally, is a parapet—a projection of the wall above the roof. Exposed on three sides, this element is exceptionally vulnerable to the effects of heat and cold and to the action of water. If it was not designed correctly or built properly, or if it has deteriorated, the parapet can be a major point of water infiltration. (Fig. I.4) And if portions of the parapet project horizontally from the plane of the façade as well as vertically, the potential for serious consequences is even greater.

Many of the problems caused by projecting façade elements can be avoided by proper detailing. The parapet, for instance, should have enough expansion joints so that repeated cycles of thermal expansion and contraction do not tear it apart. It should also be topped—as should any wall—by an impermeable coping. (Fig. I.5) Horizontal projections should have washes on their tops and drips on their bottoms to prevent water from running toward the building. Properly detailed flashing should be installed at all necessary locations. (Fig. I.6)

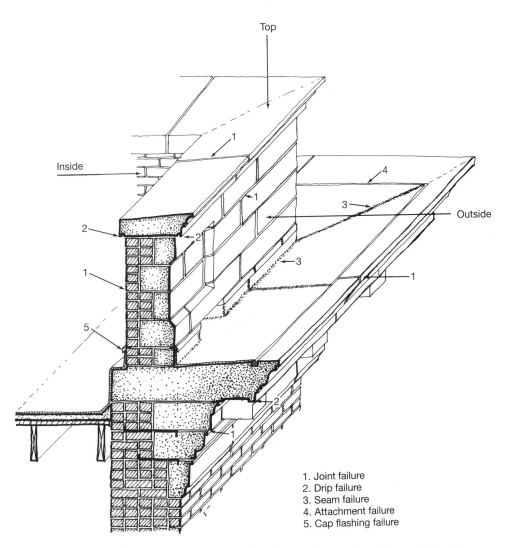

Top

Inside

Outside

1. Joint failure
2. Drip failure
3. Seam failure
4. Attachment failure
5. Cap flashing failure

FIGURE I.4. *Parapets are façade elements exposed to the weather on three sides, making them particularly susceptible to deterioration and more in need of regular maintenance. Projecting entablatures are also particularly susceptible to deterioration, failure, and water penetration.*

Gutters and Downspouts

Although not present on all building façades, gutters and downspouts can be important elements for keeping water away from the building's materials. It is common for gutters to be integrated with cornices and for downspouts to run down wall surfaces or to be concealed within the walls. Some projections, like balconies, are equipped with scuppers or drains. These elements are usually first noticed when they have not been maintained. If they are either clogged or deteriorated, water may soak areas of the façade causing

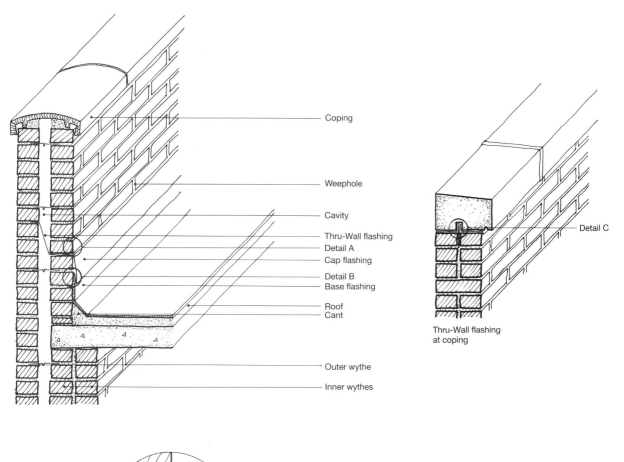

Coping

Weephole

Cavity

Thru-Wall flashing

Detail A

Cap flashing

Detail B

Base flashing

Roof

Cant

Outer wythe

Inner wythes

Detail C

Thru-Wall flashing
at coping

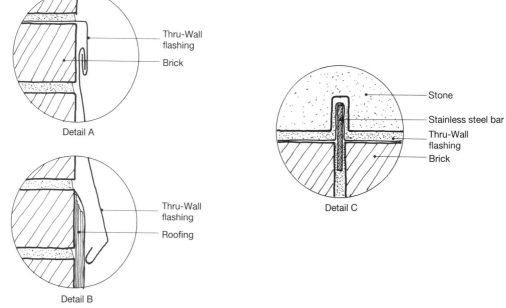

Thru-Wall
flashing

Brick

Detail A

Thru-Wall
flashing

Roofing

Detail B

Stone

Stainless steel bar

Thru-Wall
flashing

Brick

Detail C

FIGURE I.5. *Proper parapet detailing is essential to prevent water infiltration.*

FIGURE I.6. *Properly detailed flashings are necessary at interfaces between different cladding materials such as the intersection between the roof surface and the parapet wall. Patching deteriorated flashings with tar rather than repairing or replacing them can contribute to the potential for water infiltration. Cracks in the tar often allow water to penetrate the roof and enter the wall or building interior.* Sharon E. Frederick, New York Landmarks Conservancy

damage as described in the next section. It is especially important to verify that downspouts are functioning properly. If they are broken or corroded, materials in the walls may reach advanced stages of deterioration before any trouble is suspected.

DETERIORATION OF WALLS

To understand why parts of a façade deteriorate, it is necessary to know how the wall as a whole interacts with the forces that produce decay and to understand the nature of the decay itself. An effective repair and maintenance plan can be prepared only after all the causes contributing to the deteriorated condition of the façade have been determined. If damage is repaired without identifying and correcting the cause or causes of the trouble, the repair probably will not be effective, and the damage is likely to recur.

Forces destructive to a building's façade and its materials can be divided into two major categories: intrinsic processes that are a result of structural stresses and strains, and extrinsic processes that are the result of interactions between the building and its environment.

Structural Damage

Possible causes of structural damage to building façades include intrinsic causes such as improper design or siting and poor construction and extrinsic causes such as application of loads that the building was not designed to carry and changes in its surroundings.

An error in the design of a wall or its supports may mean that the building was not constructed with adequate capacity to support the loads placed on it in the first place. Although such a structure may carry these loads for a while, it may eventually fail. If the footings were not properly designed to spread the load of the wall to the soil, the building may settle into the ground. Parts of it may settle unevenly causing additional loads to be placed on some portions of the façade. (Fig. I.7) Settlement may also result if the building was improperly sited—in an area with a high watertable or above an underground stream, for example, without designing for these conditions.

A properly designed façade may fail if it was not built according to the design or specifications. Many factors resulting from poor or improper construction that contribute to the failure of walls and their components (such as failure to mix mortar properly, failure to install masonry anchors, and out-of-plumb construction) are discussed in Chapter 2. Such intrinsic flaws in construction may be exacerbated by subsequent changes in environmental conditions.

A properly designed and constructed building façade may fail because unplanned for loads have been placed on it, such as uneven settlement of the building's foundations or additions to the building that either eccentrically load or overload the wall. Other loads too great for the building might be caused by stored material, trapped water or snow, or too many occupants.

Figure I.7. *Cracked brickwork caused by uneven settlement in the foundation of the building.* James V. Banta, New York Landmarks Conservancy

While the causes of structural failure discussed are, at least to some extent, within the control of those who design, construct, and occupy the building, structural failures resulting from changes in the building's environment are often difficult or impossible to control. There are several kinds of such changes. New construction adjacent to the building may undermine its foundations or place stresses on the soil that cause a change in the way the load of the building is carried. The watertable may be lowered or raised by the action of either humans or nature. The structure may be subjected to vibrations that were not originally anticipated such as those from subsequently installed subway lines, heavy truck traffic, or pile-driving during construction on a nearby site.

Structural failures, whatever the underlying reasons, often lead to property damage and can cause loss of life. The evidence of failure may be easy to observe. A wall cracks or bows alarmingly, or part of it falls away. At the first signs of such failure, the services of a professional architect or engineer who is thoroughly familiar with the construction, materials, and structural problems of old buildings should be obtained to identify the causes of the failure and to develop solutions.

Environmental Damage

The other type of deterioration process, the interaction of the building with its environment, may have equally serious consequences, but its development may be slower and often more complex. Although wind and thermal changes can take their toll on a building's performance, water is the primary agent of environmental decay processes whether they are physical, chemical, or mechanical. Thus, the extent of the damage caused by these processes is often closely associated with two important properties of all building materials: porosity and permeability.

Porosity, Permeability, and Water in Materials. Porosity and permeability are often confused. Porosity is empty space in a substance. If these voids, or pores, are relatively large and numerous, the material is said to be porous. If the pores are connected, the substance is said to be permeable. If the pores are not connected, even a highly porous substance is impermeable. The permeability of a material also depends on the nature and type of fluid under consideration. If the pores are small enough, water droplets will not penetrate them, but relatively tiny water vapor molecules will be able to pass through quite easily. Such materials, which are water-impermeable, or "waterproof" but vapor-permeable, are sometimes called microporous.

There are five major ways water can enter a wall. It can enter from the ground or other constant source of moisture and rise by capillary action, in a process called rising damp. It can enter near the base of a wall because the improperly pitched surface of the ground around the structure directs surface water toward, rather than away from, the wall. Rainwater, other forms of precipitation, and water from other sources (such as that from improperly routed air conditioner condensate drains) can enter the wall directly through openings or porous materials. Water can also enter the top of the wall through a breach in the roof, flashings, or copings or through permeable surfaces (such as moisture entering masonry parapets unprotected by proper drips, drains, or gutters). (Fig. I.8) Finally, water vapor from the interior of the building can be drawn through the wall toward the outside face.

For a number of reasons, water may act on a façade differently today from the way it acted on the façade when the building was new. These reasons include alterations to the wall and to the means of directing water away from it such as gutters and leaders, the different environmental conditions caused by heating and cooling systems that are not original to the structure, and the addition of insulation without adequate vapor barriers or with vapor barriers that are improperly oriented. The latter two changes may create conditions that allow moisture vapor to condense in the wall.

Agents of Deterioration

The following discussion of environmental decay processes primarily concerns masonry materials. Other façade materials subject to some of the same agents will be discussed in the sections devoted to them.

Figure I.8. *On this parapet wall, the deteriorated coping, open joints in the brickwork, and failed flashings and roofing allow water to enter the wall and building interior. Deterioration can accelerate rapidly as a result of this condition.* James V. Banta, New York Landmarks Conservancy

Expansion and Contraction. Physical decay may result from mechanical action caused by the physical properties of matter. Matter expands and contracts with changes in temperature and building materials are no exception. Although dimensional changes in individual units are relatively small, the cumulative effect of such changes in a wall can be substantial. Repeated expansion and contraction alone has little effect on building components, however, if the movement is restrained in any way—by other walls or structures, for example—or if different materials expand and contract at different rates, stresses will be introduced into the wall, and façade materials may eventually become displaced, deteriorated, or broken. Relief of such stress is often evident in patterned cracks that extend through one or more components of the wall.

Water. Water, which may be present in a wall, also expands and contracts with changes in temperature. Because it has a higher rate of thermal expansion than most solids, water completely filling a pore will create pressure against the pore's walls when it expands.

Moreover, because water expands when it freezes, while solids contract, ice formation in the voids of a façade material may eventually rupture the walls of the voids. Deterioration of the material is greatly accelerated if clay minerals are present, because they swell when exposed to moisture. These processes can destroy the structural integrity of individual building blocks and of the wall itself.

Salts. Water can also contribute to the deterioration of a wall by transporting dissolved salts. Salts, the chemical compounds formed when hydrogen ions of acids are replaced by metallic ions, may be present in the components of the wall (bricks, mortar) or in materials adjacent to the wall (soil). Most salts are soluble in water and can be dissolved from their original locations and carried through permeable materials by water. Although the dissolved salts increase the volume of liquids only slightly, they can crystallize as water evaporates, and because salts in crystal form occupy more space than salts in solution, the growing crystals, if confined, exert forces on the elements confining them, such as the pore structure of masonry. The pore structure can also be broken down by crystal restructuring when some salts, such as sulfates, change their crystalline structure with changes in temperature and humidity.

The crystallization of salts can occur within the wall or on its surface. If it occurs inside the wall, it is known as subflorescence. Crystallization occurring on the surface of the wall is known as efflorescence. The presence of efflorescence on a wall shows the places where water is leaving the building and may indicate that excessive water is entering the wall at other locations. If the areas in which efflorescence occurs are not points designed for water to escape—weepholes, for example—the efflorescence may indicate unwanted openings in the masonry envelope.

Efflorescence may also indicate chemical decay. Calcium carbonate, a major component of cement mortar, limestone, and marble, is slightly soluble in water and highly soluble in acid. When water containing dissolved acidic gases from the atmosphere flows through the wall, the calcium carbonate will be leached from the mortar or stone and deposited on the surface of the wall as calcium carbonate or as calcium sulfate (gypsum), depending on the acid that dissolved it. If the calcium carbonate has been removed from the substance to the surface of the wall, the wall itself is less substantial than it should be.

Acid Rain. The presence of acid in rainwater is assured since atmospheric carbon dioxide dissolves in water to produce relatively weak carbonic acid. Much stronger acids may also be present if there are pollutants such as the oxides of sulfur and nitrogen in the air. These will dissolve in water to form very strong acids—sulfuric acid and nitric acid—which will dissolve many façade materials directly. They may also react with relatively insoluble salts to form more soluble salts. For example, sulfuric acid reacts with calcium carbonate (in marble or limestone) to form calcium sulfate (gypsum), which is between 20 and 40 times more soluble in water than is calcium carbonate. In the short term, the result of this action on a piece of stone is loss of form, rounded edges, and a crumbly surface texture; in the long term, the element disintegrates.

Biological Organisms. Growing organisms also cause environmental damage to façades. Some of these organisms, including algae, fungi, lichens, mosses, and bacteria, grow on building materials. Because they require moisture, their presence on a building is a good indication that there is too much water on or in the wall. While most of them create only superficial damage, some bacteria stimulate or accelerate chemical decay processes because they hold moisture on the wall and form acidic metabolic products.

More damage is created by higher organisms like trees, vines, and pigeons. Tree roots can break foundation walls or cause soil under footings to subside, leading to the wall's eventual collapse. Although picturesque vines add character to a wall, they grow steadily, powerfully, and relentlessly, and the roots and tendrils of many species can tear a wall apart. All vines, even those that do not penetrate the joints, shade the wall surface and contribute to keeping it constantly moist, leaving it susceptible to the usual problems of water penetration. Moreover, if vines cover a wall, the actual wall surface cannot be observed, thus inspection is difficult, and routine maintenance may not be performed.

Among the more annoying causes of biological decay in cities are pigeons. Their unsightly and alkaline droppings contain nitrates, which can attack silicate materials like glass, granite, glazed brick, and terra-cotta. The droppings also contain organic acids, which are nutrients for other organisms such as fungi. For the most part, however, pigeon droppings are more a visual nuisance and a health hazard than a serious destructive presence.

Errors of Design and Construction

In addition to all of the environmental agents that act to deteriorate walls, errors in the design or the construction of walls may cause them to fail. Although it is generally thought that buildings were constructed more soundly in the past than they are today, such was not always the case. There are many examples of poor construction in even the most elegant and impressive old buildings, including mortar joints that were not completely filled, walls that were not tied together, joints between different materials that were not properly designed, and metal anchors that corroded easily. Such conditions may increase the risk of failure in older walls.

SUMMARY

The foregoing discussion is only an introduction to the complex subject of walls and their components. They must be considered on many different levels and scales. Walls are image, object, structure, envelope, solid material, aggregations of pores, constellations of microclimates, and chemical compounds all at once. A full understanding of a façade's behavior requires a thorough investigation of all its elements and materials and of the forces acting on them.

INSPECTION

TO DETERMINE WHETHER a building façade is currently safe and whether it will be able to perform its practical and aesthetic functions in the coming years, it must be inspected. The results of the inspection, when analyzed, will determine whether the façade is in good condition and requires only regular appropriate maintenance or requires major work to make it safe and to prevent further deterioration of its materials and other building systems.

GOALS

The goals of the façade inspection should be to determine the construction of the wall (its materials and the ways they are joined, anchored, and supported); the condition of each of the materials and of their connections and supports; the reasons for any conditions indicating deterioration or failure; and possible approaches to solutions for the causes of deterioration.

APPROACH

The physical inspection of a building façade is analogous to the physical examination of a human body; the person performing the inspection must approach it in the same way that a physician approaches a person's body. Before inspecting the façade itself, it is helpful to know how it was constructed and what has happened to it during its lifetime. The history should include information about the conditions under which it was built, the forces that have acted on it, the maintenance it has received, any additions or changes made to it, and identification of the causes of, and treatments for, any previous problems.

After compiling as much background information as possible, the wall should be thoroughly examined to determine its present condition. As part of this examination, tests may be required and samples may be analyzed. If there is evidence of deterioration for which the causes cannot be determined, exploratory probes may be required. All of the information collected must be analyzed to detect patterns of deterioration and to determine the causes and severity of the wall's problems. Following this analysis, the best course of action to solve existing problems and to prevent—insofar as it is possible and practical—those that may occur in the future can be formulated. Any work carried out on the wall should be documented for the benefit of future restorers.

BACKGROUND INFORMATION

In order to fully understand a wall's present condition, it is necessary to collect all available information about its past. Collecting information on some buildings will be easy; for others, even the most persistent search will yield little. Although the value of some data will be readily apparent, the importance of other facts may not be realized until all of the information has been gathered and the building has been examined.

Among obviously significant details, for example, are the forms and materials of the anchors supporting projecting façade components. If these anchors are metal, for example, it is important to know whether they are susceptible to oxidation or galvanic action, and whether they allow for movement caused by thermal expansion and contraction or long-term water absorption. Information should also be gathered about coatings applied to the façade that might have inhibited transmission of water vapor. The fact that a wall was constructed during winter months might suggest that the mortar may not be as sound as that of a similar wall built several months earlier or later. The mortar may have been weakened by freezing before it set or by the effect of salts added to prevent the mortar from freezing.

Old photographs of the wall may show gutters and leaders that existed in the past but are no longer there. The opposite may also be true. In either case, the way water affects the wall will have changed. Photographs may also show where cracks or bulges in the masonry appeared in past years.

It is also necessary to note that information about how the façade was intended to be constructed does not mean that it was built that way. Although, for instance, drawings may show masonry ties every 16 inches, the masons may not have installed them that frequently. Likewise, not all masonry joints may have been filled as specified, and the mortar may not have been mixed as directed. Also, job conditions may have required alterations in anchoring details. Therefore, information gathered from historical sources must be confirmed by current investigation.

Sources of Background Information

Although there are many sources of historical information on a building, the owner and the local building department are the two most likely. The owner may have copies of drawings and specifications for the original construction and for any subsequent alterations, photographs showing walls at different times in the past, photographs made during construction, receipts documenting previous façade maintenance and repairs, and previous reports on the façade's condition. If the owner does not have this information in written form, he or she may at least be able to recall when the window frames were painted and caulked, when the gutters were cleaned, or when an interior leader had to be repaired because water leaking from it had damaged the plaster. The building department may have copies of original construction documents, previous reports on the façade's condition, and records of violations indicating past problems.

Other sources of information on the building include archives of the original architect's drawings and related material, city or town archives, and local libraries and historical societies. Building supervisors and maintenance personnel who have worked in the building may be able to provide valuable information. In addition to recalling work done on the façade and identifying problematic conditions that are not readily apparent, they may know whether a particular crack or bulge has been there for twenty years or has only recently appeared.

VISUAL INSPECTION

One of the most important, easiest, and least expensive methods of inspecting façades is visually—a careful examination of the wall surface making use of various commonly available tools when necessary. The visual inspection should be approached carefully and systematically. The wall should be viewed from various distances. Observations made at each vantage point will provide valuable information about the condition of the building fabric. A well-organized visual inspection can be a useful tool in diagnosing conditions; however, it cannot, in most cases, provide exhaustive conclusions.

The Overview

The first inspection should be made from a distance that allows the entire façade, or at least major portions of it, to be viewed at once. From this vantage point, it should be possible to determine major movements, failures, patterns of wear, and patterns of water penetration or waterflow across the wall. The materials of the major building elements—the skin of the wall itself and such ornamental features as portals, string courses, lintels, and cornices—should be identified. The general conditions of these elements should be observed from several vantage points. One of the first things that may be noticed is whether the wall is seriously out of level or plumb (leaning to the sides or front, or bulging in any direction). Since optical illusions occur, all visually detected deflections should be verified at close range. If any of these situations exist, it means the building has moved (most likely, settled) since it was constructed, or parts of it have moved while other parts have not, or different parts have moved different amounts. Other indications of movement are major cracks or separations in the façade.

From a distance, patterns of water movement across the façade can also be determined by observing patterns of color change in homogeneous materials, the locations of dirt on the surface, the locations of efflorescences, and patterns of streaking and staining. Inspection after a rain can be especially helpful to understanding where and how water affects the façade. Missing façade elements or parts of façade elements should be obvious even from a distance. It might also be possible to notice major areas of deterioration or abrasion of surface materials, such as the spalling or exfoliation of stone or brick.

The Close-Up View

Following the overview, the façade should be viewed at close range. While it is usually easy to get within arm's length of certain areas of the surface, such as the portion at ground level and small areas that can be examined by leaning out of windows or standing on fire escapes, it is not usually easy to examine the whole wall this closely. There is, however, no substitute for this kind of inspection. On tall buildings, the best method is to investigate the entire surface from pipe scaffolding or swing staging so that all areas can be reached and as many problems as possible exposed. Walls of shorter buildings can often be inspected from the bucket of a cherry picker. If, for reasons of cost, it is not feasible to examine the entire wall surface at close range, sample areas—those that are representative and those where special problems are known or suspected to exist—may be examined and the findings extrapolated to the entire façade.

If it is not possible to use scaffolding, staging, a hydraulic lift, or other similar means to gain access to the surface, other less satisfactory methods can be used. These methods include making a video recording of the façade (zooming in on all of the important details), photographing the façade with a telephoto lens, and, less permanently, viewing it through binoculars. None of these hands-off methods allows for as complete an examination (including such techniques as sounding materials with a hammer) as the hands-on methods just discussed. Whatever methods are used, it is necessary for the person performing the inspection to determine that they are sufficient to reveal the relevant information about the façade's condition.

This second level of visual inspection should provide detailed knowledge of the wall surface. Each element and material can be examined to determine its condition and, if it has deteriorated, the extent of deterioration. Joints between elements and materials can be checked for weather tightness. Exposed flashing can be inspected to see whether it is appropriate, sound, and properly fastened. In addition to knowledge of the visible elements, it is important to determine insofar as possible whether there is damage or indication of potential damage beneath the surface. Open joints in projecting terra-cotta, for example, indicate that the supporting members may be deteriorating even if the deterioration has not yet been made evident in splitting or separation of the terra-cotta itself. Salt deposits on the wall surface may suggest that the wall was improperly flashed or that the flashing has failed and water is entering the wall and migrating toward the exterior surface.

Common Tools to Aid in Examination

A number of tools are useful in observing the condition of a building façade. As already mentioned, binoculars allow more careful inspection of areas not accessible at close range. Although no substitute for hands-on investigation, a surprising amount of information about conditions several stories above the ground can be gained by careful and systematic observation through binoculars. A camera, too, is a useful tool. Black and white photographs are helpful in identifying patterns. Color slides are useful in making presentations on the building's condition to owners or to other members of the diagnostic team. Using a normal lens, it is possible to take overall photographs showing the building's general condition as well as more specific photographs documenting areas of special interest. A telephoto lens enables the photographing of distant conditions so that they can be studied more carefully than with the unaided eye. A macro lens permits extreme close-ups useful for documenting conditions of mortar or caulking joints and of material surfaces. A magnifying glass, of course, is also handy for examining materials in detail.

Tools that are useful in determining exactly what has happened to a building on a larger scale include a level, a plumb line, a line level, and a measuring tape or carpenter's rule (it is good to have both as each is more useful than the other in certain circumstances). Using these items, it is possible to tell whether the walls, portions of them, or other elements of a building are level and plumb or leaning, and if so, whether they are leaning in one, two, or in several directions at the same time.

More Sophisticated Aids for Examination

On large buildings and buildings where it is not possible to use the aforementioned hand tools to determine conditions, more sophisticated means can be employed to achieve the same ends. Such means include using surveying equipment or photogrammetry to provide accurate determinations of the levels and physical displacements of portions of the façade. Photogrammetry, a method providing dimensioned drawings of a façade from photographs taken by special cameras and processed using plotters or computer graphics, is more expensive than surveying. It is especially useful, however, when drawings of the façade will be required to outline work needed on the building. Photogrammetry can be used to provide information about some of the conditions of the building and to provide drawings for documenting conditions at the same time.

Recent advances in recording that can be used for examination include electronic digital cameras and video capture boards. The digital cameras record images and store them in memory. These images then can be directly transferred to a computer for analysis and incorporation in a report. Video capture boards allow individual frames from a videotape to be transferred to a computer.

PROBES

Nondestructive Probing

Although much can be learned from a visual analysis, it is often necessary to probe beneath a wall's surface to determine its condition. Methods of probing can be divided into two basic groups: those that are nondestructive to the building fabric and those that require some destruction of existing materials to provide information about interior conditions. Nondestructive methods are preferred because destructive methods leave conditions that require repair. At times, however, destructive methods will be the only realistic way to determine conditions behind the wall surface. (Fig. 1.1)

One of the simplest nondestructive probing methods is to use an acrylic-headed hammer or mallet to tap and "sound" areas of the façade. With a little experience, by listening to the sound the material makes when struck, it is possible to tell rotten from good stone, corroded sheet metal from metal in good condition, terra-cotta in which the ribs have broken off from that in which they are intact, and other differences between deteriorated and sound materials. Satisfactory conditions tend to register with a live, quick response; deteriorated conditions generally sound duller.

Another useful tool is a pen knife. By inserting the knife's tip into wood, it is possible to tell whether the wood is rotten (and if so, how deeply the deterioration exists). By scraping it across a mortar joint it is possible to tell how hard the mortar is. By prying at the edges of sealed or caulked joints, it is possible to determine whether the substance is adhering properly. By going too far with the pen knife, of course, the testing becomes destructive and repairs will be required.

A moisture meter is helpful in determining or confirming areas of the façade most subject to the action of water where that action is not visibly apparent. (Fig. 1.2) With the meter it should be easy to tell whether problems are caused by water from above, by water entering the wall around some projection or opening, or by rising damp. If the source of the water is not immediately obvious, plotting meter readings taken at regular intervals on an elevation may provide a pattern indicating the source of the problem, such as a deteriorated leader buried in the wall. Care must be taken in using the moisture meter because dissolved salts may affect the results.

FIGURE 1.1. *A borescope can be inserted into the wall cavity through a small hole in the mortar joint to view the existing conditions.* Ricardo Viera, Senior Conservator, Building Conservation Associates, Inc.

A magnet can be used to determine which of the metals used in the façade are iron or steel and thus subject to rust. A metal detector may be used to locate supporting structures, cramps, and dowels for stone and terra-cotta projections, or masonry ties. If the metal detector does not work in a particular instance, or if more detailed information is needed, other methods can be used to reveal elements within or behind the building's skin.

More sophisticated methods of nondestructive probing should be performed, and the results of the probes interpreted, by experts. Such methods include thermography, X-ray photography, ultrasonic investigation, pulse wave testing, and neutron-gamma ray analysis. Some of these methods are expensive, and all of them have limitations based on materials and access. In some instances, however, one or more of these methods and others like them may provide the only alternative to significant destruction and subsequent repair of existing building fabric.

FIGURE 1.2. *A moisture meter can help determine areas that are damaged by water where deterioration is not visibly apparent.* John H. Stahl, Stahl Restorations

Destructive Probing

When required information cannot be obtained by nondestructive probing, or when the sophisticated methods required to obtain it are not practical, it is necessary to use methods of destructive probing. The cutting of probe holes is usually done when deteriorated conditions are suspected but cannot be verified. (Fig. 1.3) It is sometimes done on large buildings to verify typical construction details. The most basic approach to destructive probing involves removing portions of façade elements, such as portions of a sheet metal cornice, or cutting holes in the fabric, such as a cavity wall, so that supporting elements and interior conditions can be examined. These activities require a qualified contractor to remove the elements and then either replace them or protect the openings. The area of the probe should be of sufficient size to allow analysis of the problem but no larger than necessary, to minimize repairs.

One of the least destructive methods of looking behind the surface of a building is the use of a borescope, a device that transmits a close-up image to the viewer along a thin tube or glass strand. This tool can be used when the area to be investigated is hollow, as within a sheet metal cornice or between wythes of a cavity wall. The borescope, which

FIGURE 1.3. *Sometimes it is necessary to cut probe holes when information cannot be obtained by nondestructive probing or when more sophisticated methods are not practical.* Raymond M. Pepi, President, Building Conservation Associates, Inc.

has its own light source, can be inserted through a small hole (about 1/2 inch in diameter). The interior of the cavity can be examined to determine the condition of anchors, flashing, and other hidden elements.

Other sophisticated kinds of probing requiring removal or alteration of existing building fabric, like sophisticated nondestructive tests, should be performed by trained professionals.

LABORATORY TESTS

In addition to tests and probes made at the building site, several kinds of tests can be performed in the laboratory when further information is required either to identify materials, to measure their properties, or to evaluate conservation or repair treatments. Relatively simple laboratory procedures determine the composition of sheet metal, the strength of mortar, and the composition of salts found on the face of a wall. Tests can also provide information about other characteristics of materials, including absorption, saturation coefficient, and freeze/thaw resistance.

After deciding that samples are required, elements for sampling should be carefully selected. Samples should be taken with as little damage to the building as possible. Architectural conservators or other specialists who will analyze the samples usually prefer to take the samples themselves so that they can observe the elements on the wall and note surrounding conditions. They can select samples in sufficient quantity for analysis from several representative locations. Each sample should be placed in its own container and identified by material and location. The locations from which samples were taken should also be indicated on drawings or photographs of the building.

Analyzing the samples in the laboratory may involve, among a great number of possible tests: examining them under a microscope to determine composition, grain structure, pore structure, and other microscopic characteristics; dissolving them in acids to separate them into their component parts, which in turn can be analyzed individually; testing them or their component parts with reagents to determine composition; and saturating them with water to determine how much they will absorb. Much more sophisticated equipment, such as an electron microscope, can be used to analyze materials and methods of deterioration. The test results must be interpreted in conjunction with all of the other information available on the structure.

LONG-TERM MONITORING

Sometimes movements of the façade or its parts are suspected but cannot be documented. At other times there is evidence of movement, but it is not known whether that movement took place in the past, and then ceased, or is ongoing. Several methods of long-term monitoring provide means for determining whether there is continuing movement in the wall.

Cracks in the wall can be measured periodically to see if they have expanded or contracted. Since movement is normally too small to be measured accurately with standard instruments such as a micrometer, a tell-tale is usually installed across the crack. The simplest tell-tale consists of two pieces of glass or plastic—one with a two-dimensional scale inscribed on it and the other with crosshairs. The pieces are glued to the wall, one fastened on each side of the crack. Any subsequent movement can be recorded by noting the position of the crosshairs on the scale. More sensitive monitoring can be done with more sophisticated gauges. (Fig. 1.4) Both tell-tales and gauges are often difficult to install across or in cracks on high-rises.

Several of the methods already mentioned as ways of discovering whether the façade is out of line can be used over time to determine whether it is moving. The relationship between a plumb bob suspended on a line hung down the façade and a stationary crosshairs can be monitored. Surveys of various points on the building or photogrammetric plots of the façade can be made at suitable intervals.

Factors other than movement can be monitored over time. Changes in the patterns

FIGURE 1.4. *A crack gauge can record minute movement over the long term.* James V. Banta, New York Landmarks Conservancy

of heat radiating from the façade, for example, can indicate changes in wetting patterns and can be compared by monitoring the structure for extended periods with time-lapse thermography.

RECORDING THE DATA

Some of the methods mentioned for observing and inspecting the building also serve as permanent records of its condition. Properly stored photographs and videotape can be reviewed years later to see what changes have taken place.

Data obtained from the façade examination should be recorded systematically to document the façade's present condition for use in the future and to provide further insight into its current problems. Recorded data enables diverse kinds of information about various parts of the façade to be compared—information such as moisture content, efflorescence, and open masonry joints.

The data can be recorded in written and graphic form. In fact, often, when examining a building, the inspector dictates into a tape recorder. If the examination has been made in a systematic manner, the transcription of this dictation will provide a clear, logical record of the conditions observed. This basic written record can be supplemented with graphics such as sketches and photographs, with captions identifying the locations and conditions shown.

The written method is satisfactory for simple buildings without serious problems, but the best method for documenting the conditions on any building is a graphic one. Information presented graphically can be related to other data and analyzed more easily than that presented in written form. An accurate elevation also serves as a base for quantity surveys, if subsequent rehabilitation work is considered.

Base Drawing

The first step in graphic recording is to obtain an illustration of the wall on which to note the information. This illustration can be produced in a number of ways depending on the size and complexity of the project and the available material. Copies of original drawings can be used if they exist; the wall can be drawn from measurements made at the site; or drawings can be made using rectified photography and photogrammetry. Photographs obtained from these processes can be reproduced and used to record the data.

Recording

Information about the façade's condition should be noted in a systematic manner. There are many ways of recording this data. A small amount of data can be noted at the sides of the elevation with arrows pointing to relevant locations. Areas of the façade that have specific problems—deteriorated joints or surface spalling, for example—can be indicated by applying tones or colors over them; a key on the drawing then indicates the significance of each tone or color. When there is more data, symbols can be used for each condition or observation. Photographs of special conditions can also be keyed to the locations of these conditions on the façade. Drawings of important details and areas can be keyed to the elevations in the same manner. The base drawing should also indicate all locations of probes, tests, and samples. This information is usually indicated with symbols.

If there is more information than can be shown conveniently on one drawing, several copies of the drawing may be used, each containing different information. It is also possible to grid the drawing and to reference information to this grid or to enlarge sections of the façade and key them into the entire façade using the grid.

No one procedure for recording information about a building façade works best in all situations. In each case, the method used should be determined after considering many factors, including the size and complexity of the façade, its condition, the availability of existing drawings, and subsequent reproductions. The goal is to produce the clearest and most complete record of façade conditions possible.

TEMPORARY PROTECTION

If any immediate signs of structural failure are noted during the inspection, temporary measures should be taken to protect persons and property from harm until the hazard has been repaired or removed. The most common form of protection is a sidewalk bridge, which allows pedestrians to walk by the structure without danger from falling objects. (Fig. 1.5) If the danger is from a specific element such as a balcony, it may be

FIGURE 1.5. *A sidewalk bridge offers necessary temporary protection for façade work.* James V. Banta, New York Landmarks Conservancy

possible to tie it to, or brace it from, another façade component. In the case of projecting elements such as cornices, nylon nets may be placed beneath them to catch any falling pieces. If there is no way to protect the public using one of these means or a similar temporary method, the element should be temporarily removed. The element—or pieces of the element, if it cannot be removed in one piece—should be labeled and stored.

Installing a means of temporary protection provides time to carefully study the problem and develop and evaluate solutions without worrying about immediate public danger. In this way, unnecessary destruction of important ornamental elements of the façade and quick, but poorly conceived, solutions can often be avoided.

PLAN OF ACTION

After the façade has been inspected and the information has been recorded, decisions about its condition and the work required to ensure that it is safe for the present and will serve its purposes in the future can be made. The façade may require only maintenance. It may only need its joints sealed, its flashings repaired, or its leaders cleaned to keep water from penetrating behind the surface. Window frames may need to be painted. Proper maintenance of the façade, although it may at times seem expensive, is the cheapest way to protect the building in the long run. If the required maintenance is deferred for financial or other reasons, small problems may become big ones, and the cost of repair will almost certainly be greater. Considerations affecting the plan for the façade are discussed next.

2

Plan for Restoration or Replacement of Façade Components

AFTER THE FAÇADE and its components have been thoroughly analyzed and all causes of deterioration have been identified, an overall plan for the repair or replacement of deteriorated components and for measures to protect the façade and its components from further deterioration should be prepared. (Fig. 2.1) Repair and replacement decisions involve many considerations. These include the extent, severity, and causes of deterioration; safety of the façade and its components; preservation of the essential aesthetic characteristics of the façade and its components; reversibility or irreversibility of repair and replacement options; availability of labor and materials; surrounding environmental conditions; and the life cycle costs of all options. Many of these factors are interrelated, and each of these factors may, in turn, involve many separate considerations.

The prime, overriding consideration when planning work on building façades is public safety. Façades must be safe for the present—there should be no loose pieces or elements that can fall off—and they must also be safe for the future—there should be no openings or deteriorated sections that will allow water to infiltrate and damage materials or corrode anchors. In addition to safety, it is important to maintain the façade's appearance, which gives it character and presence.

APPROACH TO PRESERVATION

Development of a comprehensive and coherent plan for façade conservation and restoration requires a general goal—incorporating both the requirement that a façade be safe

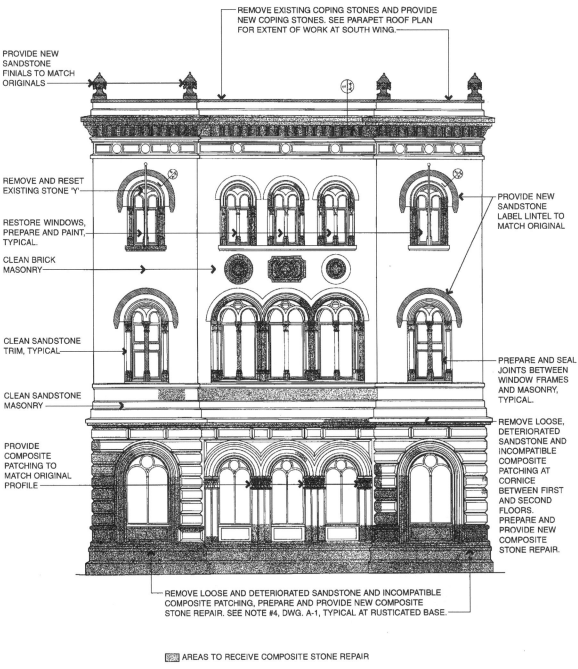

REMOVE EXISTING COPING STONES AND PROVIDE NEW COPING STONES. SEE PARAPET ROOF PLAN FOR EXTENT OF WORK AT SOUTH WING.

PROVIDE NEW SANDSTONE FINIALS TO MATCH ORIGINALS

REMOVE AND RESET EXISTING STONE 'Y'

RESTORE WINDOWS, PREPARE AND PAINT, TYPICAL.

CLEAN BRICK MASONRY

CLEAN SANDSTONE TRIM, TYPICAL

CLEAN SANDSTONE MASONRY

PROVIDE COMPOSITE PATCHING TO MATCH ORIGINAL PROFILE

PROVIDE NEW SANDSTONE LABEL LINTEL TO MATCH ORIGINAL

PREPARE AND SEAL JOINTS BETWEEN WINDOW FRAMES AND MASONRY, TYPICAL.

REMOVE LOOSE, DETERIORATED SANDSTONE AND INCOMPATIBLE COMPOSITE PATCHING AT CORNICE BETWEEN FIRST AND SECOND FLOORS. PREPARE AND PROVIDE NEW COMPOSITE STONE REPAIR.

REMOVE LOOSE AND DETERIORATED SANDSTONE AND INCOMPATIBLE COMPOSITE PATCHING, PREPARE AND PROVIDE NEW COMPOSITE STONE REPAIR. SEE NOTE #4, DWG. A-1, TYPICAL AT RUSTICATED BASE.

AREAS TO RECEIVE COMPOSITE STONE REPAIR

AREAS OF NEW STONE

FIGURE 2.1. *The kinds and scope of restoration work required on a building façade can be described on a drawing of the wall. Work described here includes masonry cleaning, stone patching and replacement, wood window restoration, painting, and caulking.* John G. Waite Associates, Architects, PLLC

and the desire to maintain the façade's appearance—against which all decisions regarding work on the façade can be measured. Although approaches to preserving and restoring old buildings vary widely, one of the most generally accepted tenets of preservation is the idea of reversibility. It is always preferable to choose a solution that can be reversed so that the original condition can be restored. A reversible procedure can be undone if it does not work, if it causes unanticipated problems, or if an improved method of restoration for this condition is found in the future. Of course, there are circumstances when the condition of the façade, the lack of available reversible solutions, or other factors, such as economics, dictate that nonreversible methods be used.

There are widely varying views of the proper way to treat landmarks—buildings of major architectural and historical significance—but there is usually a desire to preserve as much of the existing fabric as can be salvaged. According to this philosophy, deteriorated material should be patched or consolidated whenever possible, even if only a small portion of the original remains. When working with the façades of buildings that are not landmarks but are individually impressive or are important as part of a streetscape, it is usually most important to preserve the exterior appearance of the structure—the forms and profiles of its elements, the colors and textures of its materials, and the characteristics of the materials that affect their apparent colors and textures. Thus, materials should be patched if possible, and if that is not possible, should be replaced with similar materials. If changes must be made for reasons of economy or because the original materials were poor, it is sometimes possible to replace deteriorated materials with other materials that have the same form and surface characteristics without visually changing the façade's character. In all cases, the restored façade should match the original façade in color, texture, profile, and other visual characteristics.

CONSEQUENCES OF SOLUTIONS

Not all consequences of repair and replacement methods are always apparent before the methods are employed on a building. Until a material or method has been implemented, performance on the job cannot be evaluated. Thus, when new materials or methods are used for the first time, the consequences may not be fully understood. It is important, however, to use as much care as possible to ensure that proposed solutions will not result in further damage to the façade's materials or structural stability.

Failures of methods that were widely used on old buildings in the past emphasize this point. For example, many masonry buildings were cleaned by sandblasting. By removing the surfaces of the masonry units, sandblasting not only damaged the appearance of many of the materials but made them more susceptible to the action of water, thus accelerating deterioration. Silicones were applied as protective coatings to keep water from damaging façades. In some instances, instead of protecting the walls, they inhibited the passage of water vapor, and moisture trapped behind the surface led to spalling and exfoliation. Bituminous coatings, often applied to interiors of parapet walls to prevent water entry, also acted as vapor barriers, causing similar problems. Following the theory that stronger is better, hard cement mortars were used to point walls of soft brick or stone, which had originally been laid in lime mortar. Stresses from any movement caused the masonry units, rather than the mortar joints, to crack, and freeze/thaw cycles eroded the edges of the masonry rather than the mortar. In most cases, these methods were used with the best intentions but without adequate knowledge of their consequences.

FACTORS AFFECTING SELECTION OF REPAIR AND RESTORATION METHODS

Environmental Conditions

Environmental conditions are the factors over which anyone planning façade restoration and maintenance has the least control. These conditions include the direction the façade faces, which determines how much sun shines on it; the direction, strength, and frequency of the prevailing winds, which determine the action of water and airborne abrasives on it; the temperature differential and the frequency of freeze/thaw cycles; the level of the water table; and the level of pollutants in the atmosphere. Environmental factors over which there may be some control include the level of heating and air conditioning, the placement and quantity of insulation, and the location of vapor barriers. Because it is not possible to affect many of these factors, they should be carefully considered during the selection of repair and replacement options.

Materials

The availability of materials affects decisions on whether to repair or replace existing façade components. Some original materials—for example, stone from a particular quarry—may simply be unavailable. Availability is sometimes related to the quantities required. Stone from a quarry no longer worked may be available in small quantities sufficient for making dutchmen or replacing an isolated block but not for large-scale replacement. With manufactured products, on the other hand, the reverse is sometimes the case. Although it may be hard to obtain one hundred bricks to match those existing, a manufacturer might more likely accept an order for thousands of matching bricks if the ingredients were available.

Labor

Availability of labor must be considered in determining the methods to be used in restoration. There are many excellent skilled craftspeople fully knowledgeable in the handling of materials and techniques required for restoration of historic building façades, but they cannot always be found when and where they are needed. It is inadvisable to propose sophisticated procedures or techniques if workers capable of executing them are not available. It is often difficult enough to find craftspeople skilled in traditional methods of repair or restoration.

The attitude in modern construction also works against restoration projects. Too often, workers are conditioned to work against time—trying to get the job done as quickly as possible—without enough concern about the quality of the work. For example, many brick masonry façades have been permanently defaced by workers improperly removing mortar from narrow brick joints in preparation for repointing. Removing the mortar properly is a slow, monotonous procedure. It can be done efficiently, but it cannot be done hurriedly without damaging the bricks. Workers proficient in one method may not be able to adapt readily to another. Those familiar with removing soft mortar from wide masonry joints, for example, may have trouble learning how to remove hard mortar from thin joints without damage.

Scale

The scale of the repair or replacement required may affect not only the availability of materials or craftspeople and the cost of the work but also the advisability of recommending one method over another. Setup procedures and costs, for example, might make it unfeasible to replace one deteriorated terra-cotta baluster or modillion with a new terra-cotta element, although it would be feasible to use the material if a larger number of units was required. The cost of the new model and mold would be about the same for one piece as for twenty pieces. Thus, it would be much cheaper to make one piece from a material that does not shrink and can, therefore, be cast in a mold made directly from the element to be reproduced, while the cost of the model would be much less significant when spread over twenty units. As another example, it might be possible to find skilled craftspeople to do a small sandstone patching job when it would be impossible to find enough of them to patch thousands of square feet. In the latter case, cast stone produced in a factory might be a better alternative.

Quality of Original Details

In deciding whether to repair or replace, it should be determined whether the façade components and their supporting systems were properly designed in the first place. If they were not, it is necessary to determine whether the defects can be corrected by repairing the existing pieces or whether replacement would be a better solution. Among possible problems with existing components are lack of washes or drips, failure to allow for expansion, poor or improper flashings, improper support systems, and the use of incompatible materials (such as metals subject to galvanic action) in close proximity.

Compatibility of Materials

Compatibility between materials available for repair and replacement and original materials should be carefully investigated: Do the materials match the original in color and texture; do they weather in the same way, have similar permeabilities and compatible coefficients of expansion; can they be joined to each other; are they chemically compatible; and do they reflect light in the same manner?

Cost

Cost is always a consideration in façade maintenance and restoration. Many factors influence the cost, including many of the factors already mentioned. In a thorough analysis of repair or replacement costs, the initial price of the work is only one element in the equation. More important is life-cycle cost, or the cost of the proposed restoration over the life of the work performed. Comparisons of life-cycle costs may produce results different from those of the comparisons of initial costs. In addition to the initial cost of the work, the life-cycle cost of a repair takes into account the expected life of the work and all of the anticipated maintenance costs during this period.

Other factors affecting the cost of renovation include the scaffolding or swing staging necessary to reach the affected areas and to perform the work properly. In some instances, such as the composite repair of brownstone, it is preferable to use pipe scaffolding when possible to allow the work to proceed smoothly and to provide for proper supervision. The taller the building, however, the more pipe scaffolding required and the greater the project cost. The cost of the staging or scaffolding will have to be distributed over the quantity of work required.

The quantity of work, or scale of the project, will affect the cost and may make one material less expensive on a large project than another one that was cheaper on a small project. Availability of labor and materials is as much a factor as the technique specified. Work that is commonly understood, and for which the craftspeople are readily available, is usually less expensive than procedures that are uncommon and for which skilled labor is not available.

TESTING AND EVALUATION

Laboratory Testing

After preliminary solutions for repair or replacement have been selected, it may be advisable to test them in the laboratory. Replacement cast stone or polymer concrete, for example, can be tested for durability during freeze/thaw cycles, stability under exposure to ultraviolet light, hardness, water absorption, compressive strength, and other charac-

FIGURE 2.2. *Glaze repair coatings are tested to determine whether they are compatible with the properties of terra-cotta.* Ricardo Viera, Senior Conservator, Building Conservation Associates, Inc.

teristics. Coatings can be tested for adhesion, degradation under ultraviolet light, vapor permeability, and other relevant properties. (Fig. 2.2)

Site Testing

After all relevant factors have been considered and a plan for repair or replacement has been developed, it may be necessary to test the solutions or to apply sample patches on the building façade itself. It is always preferable to experiment on a small area to see whether the proposed solutions will actually work on the façade than to do large-scale work that may fail. The tests should be evaluated so that any required changes can be made before the work is carried out over the project.

REPAIR OR REPLACEMENT

Sometimes it is easy to decide whether the damaged or deteriorated façade elements can be repaired or need to be replaced. If the deterioration is minor and there are no structural consequences, repair is an obvious solution. If, however, the original material is seriously damaged, the anchors have deteriorated, and the structural system is threatened, replacement of the surface material after the anchors and structural system have been repaired or replaced is usually required.

Decisions on repair and replacement are not always so clear, of course. Many factors must be taken into account, among them: the material of the original, possible repair materials, possible replacement materials, possibility of attaching a repair, cost of repair, cost of replacement, projected life of repair, projected life of replacement, availability of materials for repair or replacement, availability of labor for repair or replacement, length of time required for production of replacement parts, location on the building, and visibility from the street.

Methods for repair and replacement of common façade components are described in the following chapters. When selecting methods for various materials, it is important to remember that the façade and its components form a system, and that the method of repair or replacement selected for one material may affect that selected for another.

STONE MASONRY

George S. Wheeler with Frances Gale
and Stephen J. Kelly

HISTORICAL BACKGROUND

FOR MILLENNIA, HUMANKIND has extracted the building blocks of its edifices from the crust of the earth. This varied and plentiful source has yielded rocks that, when fitted, shaped, tooled, and polished, become the stones of architecture. In ancient Egypt, virtually all major public buildings and monuments were constructed of stone. Dressed stonework can be seen dating from the First Dynasty, while later Egyptians joined hammer-dressed blocks with gypsum plaster. In classical and Hellenistic Greece, stone blocks were carefully worked and joined without mortar. Romans, who used stone for all major public buildings, later developed a form of construction that prefigured the development of the faced building wall in use today: walls built with a concrete core and a stone facing.

Stone continued to be a primary material in façades of great religious structures erected during the Romanesque and Gothic periods of the Middle Ages and of major palaces, civic buildings, and churches built during the Renaissance and baroque eras. Its use has continued unabated for the façades of major European buildings to the present, although now it often serves as the skin rather than as the supporting element.

In the colonial period in the United States, building in stone, with the exception of fieldstone foundation walls, was generally reserved for major civic, religious, or commercial structures. With the development of improved transportation, building stone was more readily available. Its use spread until it was a common material even for domestic buildings, as shown by the wide use of brownstone in New York City townhouses of the late 1800s. From the later years of the 19th century to the present, stone has been used as cladding on high-rise buildings of all types to convey monumentality and signify stability.

CLASSIFICATION AND PROPERTIES OF BUILDING STONES

Whether used in buildings of the Romans, the Renaissance, or the 20th century, or implemented as structure, ornament, or cladding, these stones of architecture bear evidence of their creation by one of the three rock-forming processes: igneous, sedimentary, and metamorphic. Stones formed by these processes are affected differently by environmental forces and require different cleaning and repair techniques.

Igneous Rocks

Igneous rocks are formed partly or entirely from molten material, called magma, from deep below the earth's surface. Igneous rocks are divided into two categories: volcanic and plutonic. Volcanic rocks are those that have solidified from magma issuing onto the earth's surface and cooling rapidly. The rapid cooling causes volcanic rocks to be relatively fine-grained, although large crystals—formed during periods of slower cooling before eruption—are often visible to the naked eye within their fine-grained matrices. Plutonic rocks are those that solidify slowly inside the earth and are relatively coarse-grained.[1]

Volcanic rocks are not often used for buildings in North America. In contrast, plutonic rocks such as granites are found on buildings throughout the United States and Canada. Slow cooling has caused these stones to have a high degree of crystallinity, low porosity, and high mechanical strength. Although they are formed well below the earth's surface, these rocks are ultimately made available by the erosion of more easily weathered overlying material.

Sedimentary Rocks

Rocks of the second main division, sedimentary, form in two ways. Some sedimentary rocks result from the accumulation of minerals and rock fragments, collectively called detritus, produced by the weathering and erosion of older rocks. This detritus is typically transported by water or wind and deposited far from its place of origin. The deposits or sediments comprise quartz, feldspars, micas, and clay minerals, and when compacted and lithified, constitute sandstone, one of the most common building stones worldwide. Sandstone may be classified as "siliceous, ferruginous, calcareous, or argillaceous according to whether silica, iron oxide, calcium carbonate, or clay is the predominant constituent in the matrix."[2] Other important rocks in this category are siltstone and mudstone, which are distinguished from sandstone by the smaller sizes of the detrital particles.

Other sedimentary rocks are formed not from rock and mineral debris but by the formation and precipitation of minerals within a confined area. Calcium carbonates such as calcite are by far the most abundant minerals formed by this process. While the precipitation may be an entirely inorganic chemical process, it may also be biogenic and include the accumulation of skeletons and shells, which remain visible in the compacted sediment. Cementation and lithification consists in the precipitation of additional calcium carbonate. Limestones constitute the most abundant rock type formed by these processes.

The sedimentary formation processes—the accumulation of rock and mineral detritus, of shells and marine skeletons, or of carbonate precipitates—create rocks that are more or less stratified (i.e., bedded). Compaction of these layers is dependent to a large degree on the pressures and temperatures generated by the overlying layers of sediment. The mass of overlying sediment helps to create the conditions that convert initially loose sediments into lithified rocks. The severity of these conditions, along with the nature of the cementing materials, will determine the texture and degree of stratification, the porosity, and, ultimately, the mechanical strength and durability of the resulting rocks.

Metamorphic Rocks

The third and most complex category of rocks includes those produced by metamorphic activity. Metamorphism, which brings about solid state transformations (i.e., without melting) of existing igneous and sedimentary rocks, is the result of two primary processes: the tectonic movement of large masses of the earth, which brings with it increases in both temperature and pressure; and the intrusion of molten rock, which heats nearby rocks.

The first of the processes, called regional metamorphism, takes place over large areas and often results in rocks with pronounced foliation or layering, which can frequently be seen in building stones. Important foliated rocks generated by regional metamorphism are slates, phyllites, schists, and gneisses, which are themselves distinguished by increasing grain sizes—slates have small grains, gneisses large grains, and phyllites and schists grains of intermediate sizes.

The second of these processes, called contact metamorphism, takes place over smaller areas than regional metamorphism and usually does not lead to rocks with pronounced foliation. However, the heat generated by the intrusion of magma associated with contact metamorphism usually results in increasing grain sizes in the transformation of the old rock mass to the new rock mass. Marble, which is created by the recrystallization of carbonate mineral grains in limestone, is the most commonly used building stone in this category.

QUARRYING AND SURFACING STONE

The locations of quarries and the methods used to extract stone from the earth depend on the properties of the stone being quarried. Sedimentary rocks are more easily quarried than igneous or metamorphic rocks because they can be split along the natural bedding planes and cleavage lines of the deposit. Igneous rocks, which have no uniform beds, must be hewn out in irregular blocks. Historically, small-scale quarrying was often accomplished by drilling holes in the stone along the line to be split and inserting either wood wedges, which were expanded by soaking them with water to put pressure on the stone, or two-part metal wedges, which could be driven into the holes to split the rock. The most common method of more recent large-scale quarrying is the channeling method in which a groove or trough is cut into the stone. In earlier years, this groove was cut by hand using picks and axes; later, it was cut with heavy track-mounted steam-powered channeling machines. Blocks were then split out by drilling holes along the back edge of the piece to be removed and inserting wedges as already described. In more modern quarries, after the channels have been made, the blocks are cut from the bed by wire saws, endless wires strung between pulleys mounted on frames that transport hard sand acting as a cutting agent, or diamond blades.

Blasting is often used to remove unwanted layers of rock to provide access to the desired stone. This method should not be used near high-quality stone because the force of the blast can introduce cracks and internal stresses. Unnoticed faults caused by these cracks or stresses later can lead to failure after the stone has been erected on a building façade. Much of the stone remaining in old and closed quarries has been ruined for use in buildings by improper blasting.

Stone removed from a quarry bed usually undergoes further processing. Basic methods of ancient origin still used for finishing stone blocks include hewing with an axe or pick, hammering with an axe or hammer, working with a chisel driven by a mallet or hammer, sawing, and rubbing with an abrasive. A more recent method involves passing a flame over the stone surface to spall off small portions of it, producing a rough texture, called a thermal or flame finish. In early times, the harder stones, such as granite, were generally hammered; the softer ones, such as sandstone and limestone, could be more easily hewn and chiseled. Chiseling requires more skill than using an axe or hammer because unless the chisels are handled correctly, the crystals of the stone may be crushed. Today, there is little hand tooling and finishing of stonework; most blocks are cut by gang saws into thin slabs, which are then thermally finished, honed, or polished for use as cladding.

USE OF STONE IN FAÇADES

Traditionally, stone masonry building walls served as structure—supporting not only their own weight but also loads transferred to them from floors and roofs—as well as enclosing membrane. In early stone masonry buildings, the stonework formed the full thickness of the wall. Later, dressed stone masonry was used as a facing for a core of rubble masonry or concrete. In the 19th and early 20th centuries, load-bearing masonry walls often had a stone facing with a brick masonry backup.

In stone used as a load-bearing material, the stone and the mortar in which it is set were equally important in maintaining the integrity of the structure. Mortar joints varied widely in thickness in relation to the sizes and variations in the blocks of stone being set. Rough blocks of stone required thick joints to allow for variations in the stone surfaces. Finely dressed and polished stone could be set with thin joints. The long history of using stone in building façades fostered the development of time-tested stone details, such as copings and drips, to protect the wall from water infiltration.

With the development of tall buildings and the desire to decrease the thick masonry walls necessary to support the weight of such structures, and thus reduce the cost of the cladding and increase usable interior space, masonry façade materials began to be supported by skeletal iron and steel structural frames. In the early years of this development during the late 19th and early 20th centuries, stone masonry was supported on the frame at every story or two; the masonry had to support its own weight between supports. On high-rise buildings today, stone is almost always used as a nonload-bearing cladding material, supported completely by the building's structural frame.

In buildings with skeletal frames there were several means of attaching the stone cladding to the structural elements. If the cladding had a masonry backup—a layer of brick or tile behind it—cramps were often installed at the top of every slab to attach the stone to the backup. Dowels were used to anchor the bottom of each stone slab to the one below and sometimes to align the slabs horizontally as well. At other times, the horizontal alignment was accomplished with joggles—male and female alignments carved into the blocks themselves. Corrugated ties provided another method for anchoring stone veneer to masonry backup. The veneer could also be supported on metal angles, which were attached either to the backup masonry or directly to the structural skeleton.

Sometimes the individual stone blocks of projecting façade elements—of cornices for example—could be anchored in much the same manner as those of the flat portions. Elements of cornices that did not project too far could sometimes be counterweighted by masonry above them. When counterweighting was not possible or the projection was too great, the cantilevered masonry was anchored by rods or bolts tying it to the remainder of the wall or by metal supports attached to the structural frame. Elaborate iron or steel anchoring systems were devised to support heavy projecting elements such as cornices and balconies.

During the early development of high-rise construction, lack of experience with curtain walls and lack of knowledge about the behavior of materials caused designers and builders to make mistakes in several major areas—mistakes that have affected the conditions of many tall buildings. These areas include the anchoring system, the treatment of joints in the exterior skin, and the failure to provide appropriate means for water to pass out of the wall.

In the first instance, anchoring devices (including cramps, dowels, and ties) and relieving angles were often made of unprotected iron or steel. Rusting anchors and supports that led to cracked stone blocks, and, ultimately, failure of the cladding exposed the drawbacks of using these materials. Today, in most cases, anchoring devices are made of galvanized or otherwise protected ferrous metals, stainless steel, nonferrous metals, and certain plastics.

In the second instance, designers did not understand the consequences of the different thermal qualities of the metal skeleton and the stone cladding, or of the thermal movement of large expanses of the cladding itself. In many cases, all of the joints in the cladding were of mortar, which could not absorb the movement of the blocks of stone as the skeleton expanded and contracted. Joint failures in these façades led to the use of flexible joints in both horizontal and vertical directions. Today, horizontal control joints are used to allow the exterior skin to maintain its integrity even when the skeleton behind expands and contracts or deflects (because of wind loading, for example); vertical control joints are used to absorb the expansion and contraction of large expanses of the cladding material itself, and to prevent the material from being restrained at the corners or by vertical structural members.

The third common failure in early high-rise development was the lack of proper flashing and weepholes at lintels over masonry openings and at relieving angles, which prevented water entering the wall or condensation forming in the wall from passing to the exterior. The water retained in the wall led to deterioration of ferrous anchors and supports. Today, proper design of masonry cladding provides for flashing and weepholes above all openings and over all supports.

DETERIORATION AND EVALUATION OF STONE MASONRY

The condition of stone used on façades must be analyzed, along with the condition of the wall as a whole, to determine if it is sound or deteriorated. If deterioration has occurred, the severity of the failure and its causes must be determined before decisions about repair or replacement can be made, in order to preclude further deterioration.

The lowest level of deterioration is surface erosion, where only the appearance of the stone's surface is damaged. Exfoliation, cracks and splits, joint failures, missing sections, and deteriorated anchors are more severe because they affect the structure of whole stone blocks. Failure of the supporting structure is the most severe failure because it threatens the façade's structural stability.

Deterioration of stone masonry may involve the mortar joints as well as the stone. Causes of mortar deterioration are covered in Chapter 7.

Deterioration of Building Stone Related to Its Properties and Its Environment

From the time rocks were first exposed on the earth's surface, they have been affected by wind, rain, changes in temperature, and aggressive fluids. The effects of these forces on stone are often collected under the term weathering. Most of these same agents of weathering cause changes to building stones similar or identical to those of rock outcrops. Unlike rock outcrops, however, buildings are artificial constructs with defined relationships to prevailing winds, to rainfall, to the movement of water across and down their surfaces and forms, and to groundwater. Because of these relationships, weathering processes on buildings may differ in form, extent, and intensity from these same phenomena in a natural setting, and, therefore, will hereafter be referred to as processes of "deterioration."

Deterioration of building stone may arise due to the intrinsic properties of the rock from which the building stone was created or to extrinsic factors including changes brought about in the transformation from rock to building stone, position on the building, and the nature of the surrounding atmosphere. (Fig. 3.1) Often, both intrinsic and extrinsic factors are involved. The deterioration of exposed stone can generally be attributed to the following processes:

FIGURE 3.1. *This sandstone lintel has deteriorated because it was face-bedded, or installed with the bedding planes parallel to the façade. The natural layers of the stone are more prone to mechanisms of deterioration such as freeze/thaw cycles.* Dean Koga, Project Manager, Building Conservation Associates, Inc.

salt crystallization: The disruptive forces (i.e., physical) due to the formation and growth of crystals at the surface.

acid rain and dry deposition: The etching, leaching, or dissolution (i.e., chemical) of one or more mineral constituents due to the action of acidic solutions.

thermal effects: The mechanical stresses (i.e., physical) accompanying the freezing of water in pores, cracks, and channels in the stone and cracks arising from heating and cooling of the stone surface.

biodeterioration: The physical and chemical consequences of the interaction of biological species with stone such as bacteria, algae, fungi, lichens, mosses and higher plants, and birds and other mammals.

wetting and drying: The mechanical stresses and changes in dimension (i.e., physical) that occur when water enters and later exits the porous network of stone.[3]

Salt Crystallization. Salts generally make their presence known on a building as efflorescences. These fine white crystals present on the surface of the stone indicate that the crystallization is also taking place below the surface, a phenomenon often referred to as subflorescence but more accurately described as subsurface crystallization. Subflorescences cause damage to stone in the form of granular disintegration, or sugaring, which is a loosening of individual grains at the stone's surface.

When salts are present, their identification may also help to determine their sources. If salts and the sources of salts are not removed, they will continue to cause deterioration. Table 3.1 lists the most common salts found on buildings, along with their sources.

Acid Rain and Dry Deposition. Deterioration of building stone by acid rain is an example of the ill-fated meeting of intrinsic properties and extrinsic factors: carbonate rocks such as limestone and marble invariably comprise calcite, a mineral readily soluble in acid. Natural rainfall, of course, is slightly acidic due to normal levels of carbon dioxide in the atmosphere. However, greater consumption of fossil fuels, which began with the Industrial Revolution and increased dramatically after World War II, has led to ever-increasing acidity of rainfall in many areas. This added acidity stems not so much from carbon dioxide but from sulfur dioxide generated by impurities in oil or coal. Through a complex set of chemical reactions, sulfur dioxide combines with atmospheric water and other gases to form sulfurous and sulfuric acids. Upon contact with limestone or marble, these acids cause direct deterioration by dissolution of calcite. This damage manifests itself as granular disintegration with attendant loss of surface detail and reduced mechanical strength to depths of 1 to 2 inches from the outer surface. A by-product of this reaction is calcium sulfate in the form of gypsum, which can later cause damage by salt crystallization.

Gypsum can also form by a second mechanism called dry deposition. This process

Table 3.1. COMMON SALTS FOUND ON BUILDINGS AND THEIR SOURCES
by George Segan Wheeler

Chemical Symbol	Chemical Name	Mineral Name	Sources
NaCl	sodium chloride	halite	deicing salts, marine aerosol
CaCl$_2$ or CaCl$_2$·6H$_2$O	calcium chloride —hexahydrate	antarticite —	deicing salts deicing salts
Na$_2$SO$_4$ or Na$_2$SO$_4$·10H$_2$O	sodium sulfate —decahydrate	mirabilite thenardite	portland cement or alkali cleaning products
CaSO$_4$·2H$_2$O	calcium sulfate dihydrate	gypsum	limestone, marble, concrete, or lime mortars
CaCO$_3$	calcium carbonate	calcite	dissolution and redeposition of calcium carbonate from concrete and lime mortars
NaHCO$_3$ or Na$_2$CO$_3$ or Na$_2$CO$_3$·10H$_2$O	sodium bicarbonate sodium carbonate —decahydrate		concrete concrete concrete
NaNO$_3$	sodium nitrate	soda niter	decomposition of organic materials, biological growth
MgSO$_4$·6H$_2$O	magnesium sulfate hexahydrate	hexahydrite	magnesium carbonate or calcium-magnesium carbonate (i.e., dolomite) from dolomitic limestones, marbles, or lime
MgSO$_4$·7H$_2$O	magnesium sulfate heptahydrate	epsomite	

requires no actual precipitation—hence the name dry deposition—and involves the interaction of sulfur dioxide with wet or damp stone surfaces. The reaction occurs when sulfur dioxide gas meets the film of water on the carbonate stone surfaces. (Fig. 3.2) This reaction appears to be catalyzed by porous carbon particles and iron oxides often found as soiling on these same surfaces. The gypsum resulting from dry deposition tends to form relatively thin layers (less than 1 millimeter) and can provide a protection to the stone surface for some time. However, as time passes, wetting and drying brings about damage by salt crystallization; therefore, it is usually advisable to remove gypsum in this form.

Freezing Water. It has long been observed that freezing water damages rock outcrops and building stones alike, but the mechanisms of deterioration by this process are not firmly established. The 10 percent increase in volume that water experiences upon freezing surely contributes to the deterioration of stone. In this case, the mechanism is simply the attempted expansion in a confined space, much like water freezing in a bottle.

FIGURE 3.2. *Gypsum crusts can form when the wet surface of carbonate stones comes in contact with sulfur dioxide gas in the atmosphere.* Ricardo Viera, Senior Conservator, Building Conservation Associates, Inc.

The severity of damage depends on the level of saturation of the stone by water and the ability of the stone to withstand the resulting pressures, that is, the mechanical properties of the stone. Other mechanisms often cited are hydraulic pressure generated by the compression of unfrozen water in narrow pores and the formation of ice crystals in large pores, which are fed by liquid water in smaller pores causing further growth of the ice crystals. In these latter two mechanisms, both the mechanical properties of the stone and the distribution of pore sizes within the stone influence the level of damage: stones with small pores connected to large pores would appear to be susceptible to damage by these mechanisms.

It is difficult to assess on a particular building which of these processes are involved. Nonetheless, both field experience and laboratory testing indicate that stones, regardless of type, that are more saturated with water—80 to 90 percent—are more liable to be damaged by freezing. The position of a stone on a building in relation to sunlight (i.e., drying by insolation), ground water (i.e., rising damp), prevailing winds, and rain strongly influence the level and duration of water saturation. Clearly, the maintenance of a building's water management systems affect the level of saturation and therefore the degree of freezing damage a particular stone sustains. Mechanically weaker stones and stones with prominent bedding planes are less able to withstand the pressures resulting from any of the mechanisms of freezing water. These stones include many sedimentary rocks such as limestones and sandstones. Many plutonic and metamorphic rocks (granites and marbles) commonly used as building materials are less susceptible to frost action due to their higher mechanical strengths.

Wetting and Drying. As a footnote to freezing water damage to stone, it should be pointed out that simple wetting and drying can cause irreversible damage that is often mistakenly diagnosed as caused by freezing water or salt crystallization. Stones such as argillaceous sandstones, which are porous, prominently bedded, mechanically weak, and contain clay, appear to be susceptible to this process.

Biodeterioration. Biological agents also contribute to the deterioration of stone. While only in recent years have the specific processes and mechanisms become better understood, the importance of biological agents in the production of soil by the breakdown of rocks has long been recognized. Active soil formation bears evidence for the fact that, although these biological deterioration processes may, at times, be slower and less dramatic than acid rain and freezing water, they can be potent agents of stone disintegration. The modes of disintegration are both physical and chemical and are affected by several genera: bacteria, algae, lichens, fungi, mosses and other higher plants, as well as birds and other mammals.

Bacteria. Bacteria are microorganisms, which cannot be detected with the naked eye. Their effects on stone, however, can be readily noticed. Although bacteria have little mechanical effect on stone, the chemical effects related to the microorganisms are damaging.

The dominant chemical agents in the deterioration of stone by bacteria are acids. Through respiration alone and the attendant production of carbon dioxide, bacteria can generate sufficient quantities of carbonic acid to digest acid-sensitive materials such as limestone and marble. Metabolites of bacteria can also be organic acids other than carbonic that are potent mineral digestives. Acidic metabolites that are neutralized in their environments can continue to produce damage in stone by chelation—a process in which selective elements are extracted from minerals.

Sulfur- and nitrogen-fixing bacteria are responsible for the production of inorganic (mineral) acids such as nitric and sulfuric. These acids are well known for their ability to dissolve carbonate and, to some degree, other minerals.

Bacteria can also produce alkalis, which can dissolve the silicate minerals comprising many stones such as granite, sandstone, schist, and gneiss. Various types of bacteria are oxidizing agents, which will cause staining in stones that contain iron or manganese.

Algae. Unlike bacteria, algae can often be detected on stone by the naked eye. Algae form a gelatinous skin—referred to as biofilm—that expands and contracts when in contact with water and under conditions of drying. Mineral grains may be extracted as the biofilm expands and contracts. The gelatinous sheaths retain water, which allows other forms of deterioration involving aqueous media—such as acid rain, dry deposition, freezing water, and salt crystallization—to persist.

Algae have numerous chemical effects. As with bacteria, simple respiration of organisms produces carbonic acid. Metabolic processes generate organic acids such as aspartic citric, glutamic, glycollic, oxalic, and uronic, all of which can cause significant damage to stone. When neutralized, these organic acids also act as chelators of selected elements in minerals.

Fungi. Fungi often appear as a velvety growth, either white or colored and are sometimes accompanied by a musty odor. In advanced stages of growth, fruiting bodies of fungi may resemble mushrooms. An important feature of fungal growth is their hyphae, threadlike growths, which may penetrate into the porous network of stone. Hyphal penetration carries with it mechanical stresses, which may disrupt and loosen grains of stone in the growth process.

Fungi are also responsible for chemical deterioration of stone in ways similar to those caused by bacteria and algae. Respiration produces carbonic acid along with metabolic organic acids such as oxalic, lactic, gluconic, glucoronic, and fumaric, which dissolve carbonate minerals and extract silicon, iron, magnesium, and calcium from rock-forming minerals. In their neutralized forms, these acids remain potent chelators. Inorganic acids such as nitric and sulfuric are formed by fungi-generated oxidative processes.

Lichens. Lichens are a group of plants consisting of two unrelated components, fungi and algae, living in a symbiotic association.4 The vegetative plant body, referred to as the thallus, that results from this relationship bears little resemblance to either of its "parents." Lichenous growth forms consist of three classes: crustose, foliose, and fructicose. All forms grow slowly but are resistant; their appearance on stone may be quite dramatic.

Lichens are also characterized as epilithic, in which hairlike rhizoids nourish themselves at the expense of the stone; and endolithic, in which the thallus is inside the stone, and its fruiting body, when large enough, appears on top of the stone surface. Some lichens (calcicolous) prefer carbonate rocks, and some (silicolous) prefer silicate rocks.

It has been suggested that lichens may be protective to stone because their covering is so complete, although there is not a consensus on this point. Lichens can retain water, which may accelerate or promote water-related deterioration processes. Mechanical damage to stone may result from rhizoid penetration, as well as from the expansion and contraction of the gelatinous biofilm. This expansion and contraction may cause detachment of the thallus, which may pull mineral grains with it.

Chemical effects resulting from lichens are similar to those resulting from bacteria, algae, and fungi. Respiration produces damaging carbonic acid, and metabolism generates organic acids including oxalic, citric, salycic, tartic, and gluconic. In neutral forms, these acids serve as efficient chelators. Lichens also produce polyphenolics, which are powerful chelators.

Mosses and Higher Plants. Although mosses are a familiar form of biological growth, they represent a large and complex group of plants, which are rather drought-resistant. They appear to have little mechanical effect on most stones, but they do retain moisture. Their chemical action consists in secretion of acids at root tips, suckers, and tendrils, as well as the chelation power of the neutralized acids.

Unlike mosses, higher plants such as ivy, creeper, and even trees can cause severe mechanical damage. Ivy and creeper can attach to stone surfaces, and their attachments may penetrate and then detach mineral grains. As the trunks of these plants (or trees) grow large, they may lift even several hundred pounds of stone. Like mosses, they cause chemical damage by the secretion of acids at root tips, suckers, and tendrils. These secretions dissolve minerals and aid in the attachment of the plant material to the stone surface and the penetration of the plant material beneath the stone surface.

Birds and Other Mammals. Birds and other mammals may cause mechanical damage to the surfaces of stone as they move on and across stonework. They may also leave stains on stone surfaces. The most important mode of deterioration for these mammals is the guano they leave behind, often in great abundance. The guano not only soils and stains stone surfaces, but it contains or produces nitric, phosphoric, and uric acid, which can cause direct damage. Guano may also contain damaging salts, or neutralized acids may form salts, which will continue to cause deterioration. Guano is also an excellent nutrient source for other biological species, encouraging them to take hold and flourish.

Deterioration Related to Quarrying and Working Stone

Humankind may also contribute to the future deterioration of stone during its quarrying, working, and installation. Removal of large quarry blocks with pneumatic hammers or small dynamite charges rather than with hammers and large chisels may introduce a network of microcracks. The presence of these microcracks reduces the mechanical strength of the stone and increases its porosity. The increased porosity allows for liquids to penetrate more easily and in greater volumes, and thus makes these stones more susceptible to deterioration by acid rain, freezing water, wetting and drying, and salt crystallization. Biological agents also have a larger network of pores into which hyphae and tendrils may penetrate. Bush hammering of stone surfaces can also increase the porosity of the surfaces, and even greater damage can result when the bush hammering is done with pneumatic tools. This surface porosity creates greater access for both water and acid rain, as well as reactive acid-generating gases such as sulfur dioxide and nitrogen oxides.

Deterioration Resulting from Improper Details and Specifications

Some of the most common problems associated with improper detailing and specifications are those that allow water to enter the wall and those in which the anchoring system was improperly designed. Both of these conditions have been discussed.

The most common misuse of stone in the process of installation is face-bedding, placement of a stone on a building with the plane of sedimentation (i.e., bedding) parallel to the plane of the façade. This kind of placement is tempting because stone is easier to dress along the bedding planes. However, scaling and exfoliation often result.

Failure of bearing masonry may have been caused by failure to specify the proper mortar or the proper conditions at time of installation as discussed in Chapter 7, Mortar.

Early stoneclad skeletal frames have often failed because the original designers and builders did not understand all of the ramifications of this new type of construction. The use of unprotected ferrous metal for supporting and anchoring devices (such as lintels, relieving angles, and ties between wythes) led to rusting supports and anchors and, eventually, façade failures. (Fig. 3.3) Lintels and relieving angles were installed without proper flashing or weepholes to allow water to drain from the wall, thus allowing water to accumulate inside the cavity where it could accelerate deterioration of ferrous metal and saturate masonry, leading to freeze/thaw damage. Walls were also clad without flexible joints able to absorb the differential thermal movement that might take place between the metal skeleton and the brick masonry or the thermal movement of large expanses of the masonry itself.

Where stone masonry was used as an exterior cladding supported on the building's structural system, failure may have occurred because of inadequate support, anchoring, or provisions for relieving stress. Supports may not have been protected sufficiently from water. Corroded iron or steel anchors may have expanded sufficiently to crack the wall. Early, anchors often were not installed as frequently as they should have been. The cumulative weight of an inadequately anchored wall may cause areas of the masonry to buckle outward. Even if the anchors were installed where required, it is possible that they have deteriorated. It is also possible that the original construction did not provide sufficient provisions for movement of the masonry elements—a

FIGURE 3.3. *Corroded supports can lead to the failure of stone elements such as this limestone bracket.* Raymond M. Pepi, President, Building Conservation Associates, Inc.

requirement especially important in multistory structures. Where the masonry was too rigidly connected to the metal supporting structure, substantial vertical cracking may have occurred to relieve the stresses caused by thermal movement. This cracking accelerates weathering and deterioration.

Steel, concrete, and stone masonry all have different thermal coefficients: they change dimensions in different amounts and at different rates with fluctuating temperatures. These different dimensional changes may have led to the cracking of a masonry wall if differential movements caused by variations in temperature were restrained by an inflexible anchoring system or by the absence of expansion joints or inadequate expansion joints. Symptoms of this condition are patterned cracks appearing at corners, piers, or other locations where the mass of the wall changes.

Uneven settlement caused by improperly designed foundations, or by changes in subsurface conditions or loading after construction, may have caused cracking in stone masonry. Inadequate detailing of the structure, too, may have led to other damage of masonry walls. If adequate flashing at the roof line and other systems to convey water away from the wall were not provided as discussed, serious damage may have occurred.

Deterioration Resulting from Improper Workmanship

Failures resulting from poor workmanship include failure of mortar because it was not properly proportioned or not adequately mixed, or because it was retempered too many times before it was installed. It is also possible that the mortar joints were not properly made. Mortar may not have been applied over the full surfaces of the stone blocks. If mortar was applied only near the edges, the joints may be weak and susceptible to water penetration. The head joints may not have been completely filled with mortar, leading to similar problems.

Other problems caused by poor workmanship include fewer anchors or fasteners than required, and cavities partially filled with mortar droppings and debris.

Deterioration Resulting from Improper Maintenance

One of the most common forms of improper maintenance leading to future stone deterioration is the use of mortar that is harder and more vapor-impermeable than the stone. Such mortar restricts the passage of moisture and salts through the joints and causes them to pass through the stone.

Application of water-vapor-impermeable coatings in the past may have caused damage to the stone masonry. Coatings containing silicone, finely ground cement, or bituminous compounds have often been applied to stone masonry with the intention of preventing water from entering the wall. However, water can enter the wall in locations other than those covered with the coating or in gaps or deteriorated areas of the coating. Typical locations of such water entry include failed flashings, deteriorated copings, open sealant joints, and areas near the base of the wall subject to rising damp.

Moisture often enters a wall from the interior of the building and condenses in the masonry. Water entering the wall behind the surface coating may contain soluble salts or dissolve soluble salts from the masonry. The salt solution may then migrate toward the barrier, and the salts may crystallize behind it. This disruptive force may break the coated face away from the masonry unit. Damage can also result from expansion of condensed water passing through freeze/thaw cycles. If a relatively vapor-impermeable coating was applied over an entire masonry wall and any water was able to enter, salt crystallization or freeze/thaw cycles can cause severe damage to the masonry.

REPAIR OF STONEWORK

Important aspects of the restoration of stone façades are the replacement, or introduction wherever possible, of flashings and damp-proofing courses, and proper stone details such as projections and drips to keep water from running over the surface of the wall and entering it. Often, the stone itself must be repaired. Repairs may be minor, involving resurfacing, patching, or consolidation, or major, involving the repair of anchoring systems or the replacement of individual blocks of stone.

Consolidation

Stone surfaces exhibiting granular disintegration (sugaring) or crumbling, can sometimes be consolidated to renew the mechanical strength of the deteriorated stone. Sugaring stems from the loosening of individual mineral grains as a result of mechanical stresses, dissolution along grain boundaries, or a combination of both. While virtually any stone may exhibit sugaring or crumbling, sandstones, limestones, and marbles are most susceptible and, therefore, the most frequent candidates for consolidation.

Consolidation treatments are documented from as early as Roman times when drying oils, waxes, and hide glues were applied to stone.[5] Lime water—saturated solutions of lime—has also been used since ancient times and continues to be used today for limestones and, in some cases, marbles. After World War II, many consolidation treatments involved the application of modern synthetic resins such as acrylics, epoxies, polyesters, and polyethylene glycol. The 1960s witnessed the birth of two new consolidants: alkoxysilanes[6] and barium hydroxide-urea.[7] In current restoration practice in the United States, alkoxysilanes prevail, with epoxy and acrylic resins a distant second.

Consolidation treatments appear to function in two ways: forming adhesive bridges between and among loose mineral grains—essentially gluing mineral grains together; and filling (or partially filling) the interstices of loose mineral grains—mechanically locking mineral grains in place. Each of the organic resin-based systems follows the first mechanism, adhering grains together. In limestones or marbles, lime water and alkoxysilanes function by the second mechanism, precipitating calcium carbonate or silica gel, respectively, between grains of calcite. On sandstones, it has been suggested that alkoxysilanes form adhesive bridges between grains of silicate minerals and thus would follow the first mechanism.

The adhesive mechanism is important in securing mineral grains both on sugaring and crumbling stone. Lacking that adhesive capability, alkoxysilanes and lime water do not perform this grain-securing function on limestone and marble nearly as well as acrylics (or acrylic-silicone) and epoxies. While these resins also generally outperform alkoxysilanes on sandstones as well, the disparity is not nearly as great as it is on limestone. Based on the ability of acrylics, acrylic-silicones, and epoxies to increase mechanical strength in crumbling stone and secure mineral grains in sugaring stone, it would seem that there would be no reason to use other materials. However, organic resins can break down when exposed to the ultraviolet component of solar radiation, while the consolidating gel formed from alkoxysilanes has superior stability to solar ultraviolet.[8] Thus, some stone conservation practitioners have come to accept the less than ideal performance by alkoxysilanes in reducing sugaring or increasing mechanical strength as a trade-off for their superior light stability. Alkoxysilanes are pervasively used on sandstone and increasingly on limestone and marble.

Before a stone consolidant is selected or applied, conditions must be carefully evaluated to ensure that the chosen consolidant will adequately penetrate the stone and have no adverse effects on the stone, anchoring systems, and other façade materials.

Stone consolidants are difficult to apply, particularly on building façades. As all consolidants require stone that is dry, large areas of a façade must often be covered for several days or longer before treatment can safely be executed. The application process is often slow, requiring the use of brushing or spraying, and involves the use of flammable solvents;[9] multiple applications are sometimes necessary. In the case of the most widely used alkoxysilane consolidant in the United States, nine to fifteen applications can be required, depending on the porosity of the stone. The applications must be executed on a fixed schedule. Consolidants often have upper and lower limits of temperature and relative humidity during their application; this is particularly true of alkoxysilanes. All organic resin systems and, at times, alkoxysilanes require removal of excess surface material after application to prevent the formation of a "glazed" finish. In addition, some consolidants can permanently change the hue or value of the stonework; some changes may not be permanent but may nonetheless alter the appearance of the stone for several months before the stone returns to its original appearance. After the application process is complete, little work can be done on completed stonework for up to several weeks, and the treated areas must be protected from the weather during this period. Cement-based pointing or patching materials cannot be applied to stone that has been treated with organic resin systems or hydrophobic alkoxysilane systems; at least one month must pass before they can be applied to nonhydrophobic alkoxysilane systems.

All of these factors taken together often make it difficult to schedule the application of consolidants or schedule other work around their application. Scheduling problems, the expense of the material, safety considerations, and the need to have trained conservators select, evaluate, and supervise the use of consolidants and skilled craftspeople to apply them make the use of consolidants a generally complicated and expensive procedure. Consolidants do, however, have a place in the treatment of sugaring and crumbling building stone. Such treatments must be carefully tested and well thought out before they are carried out on a building façade.

Stonework Repair Methods

Retooling. When weathering and decay of a stone masonry façade is uniform, and not too deep, surfaces of the individual stone blocks can sometimes be satisfactorily redressed with a chisel to remove flaking and deteriorated stone from the surface, improving the appearance and safety of the façade. Care must be taken not to use this method when the new surface of the block will be more than 3/8 inch behind the plane of the façade. Deeper recesses may provide ledges for standing water. Even if the new surface is within 3/8 inch of the façade plane, the ledge below the block should be given a wash so that water will not sit on it or run back toward the joint.

Composite Patching. When areas of stone surfaces have exfoliated and decayed to the point where neither consolidation nor resurfacing is effective, and when small portions of blocks have been damaged, composite patching may be used to reconstruct them. Although this method has been tried on many types of stones, it is most appropriate for those with fairly uniform faces such as sandstone, limestone, and some types of marble; (Fig. 3.4) it is generally less successful on granite. Composite patching is not usually used to repair large uninterrupted areas, but is commonly implemented in small areas of flatwork and projections. Unanchored composite patching should be limited to patches less than 2 inches thick. Using this technique, missing stone faces and modest-sized projections are duplicated through a series of stuccolike applications of mortar

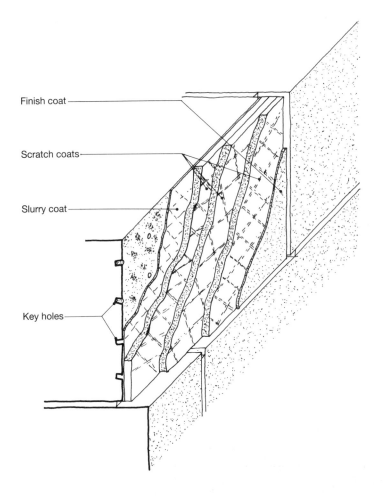

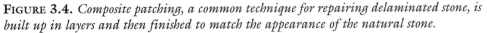

FIGURE 3.4. *Composite patching, a common technique for repairing delaminated stone, is built up in layers and then finished to match the appearance of the natural stone.*

mixes. The final application is treated to match the form and dressing of the original surface. Care must be taken to match the appearance of the old stone, and in mixing, applying, and finishing the repair material. The patching mixture should weather in the same way as the original stone.

Several proprietary cementitious patching compounds are available. These come ready-mixed, requiring only the addition of water. They can be supplied in custom colors to match to the color of the stone on the building. They are often applied by masons trained by the manufacturer. A standard job-mixed repair mixture consists of a cement and lime binder, crushed stone and sand aggregate, and small amounts of dry oxide pigments as necessary to achieve the proper color. Great care should be taken to match the color, aggregate size, and texture of the surrounding stone. Color matching should always be to the color of the clean stone, even if the remaining original stone is not going to be cleaned at the time of the repair; there is always the possibility that it will be cleaned in the future. As with the proprietary patching mixes, it may be necessary to use several colors to match the variations in the colors of the stone blocks on the façade. Color should be achieved as nearly as possible with the aggregates so that only small amounts of pigment are required. Acid rain may dissolve the binder and pigment over time. If the color of the aggregate is not nearly the same as the final surface color, the color of the patches may change appreciably as the binder and pigment are washed from the surface. It may also be necessary to add other elements, such as mica, to the mix to duplicate characteristics of the original stone. After the dry ingredients have been thoroughly mixed, they may be combined with a mixture of water and acrylic latex admixture.

The loose and crumbling surface of the stone to be treated should be cut back to sound stone with a toothed chisel, leaving a rough surface. The edges of the area to be repaired are then slightly undercut to provide keys for the patch. Splayed holes should be drilled in the base to provide additional keys for the new material. The cement mixture is applied to sound stone in layers. A slurry coat is followed by several scratch coats and a final finish coat. The surface of the finish coat is treated to match the surface of the surrounding stone by one of several methods, including rubbing and acid etching.

Dutchmen. Dutchmen repairs are useful for replacing small missing or deteriorated sections of stone. First, the area of replacement should be neatly trimmed and squared. An insert of either matching natural stone or a compatible cast stone facsimile should be cut to size and surfaced to match the existing material. After the dutchman has been fit, it should be wedged in place and bonded with an appropriate adhesive, which must be unaffected by water and compatible with the stone and the patch. Tooling and surfacing may also continue after installation of the dutchman. (Fig. 3.5)

Anchored Dutchmen. Where large pieces of a block are cracked or broken away (pieces of twelve square inches or larger), large dutchmen can be inserted. Unlike small dutch-

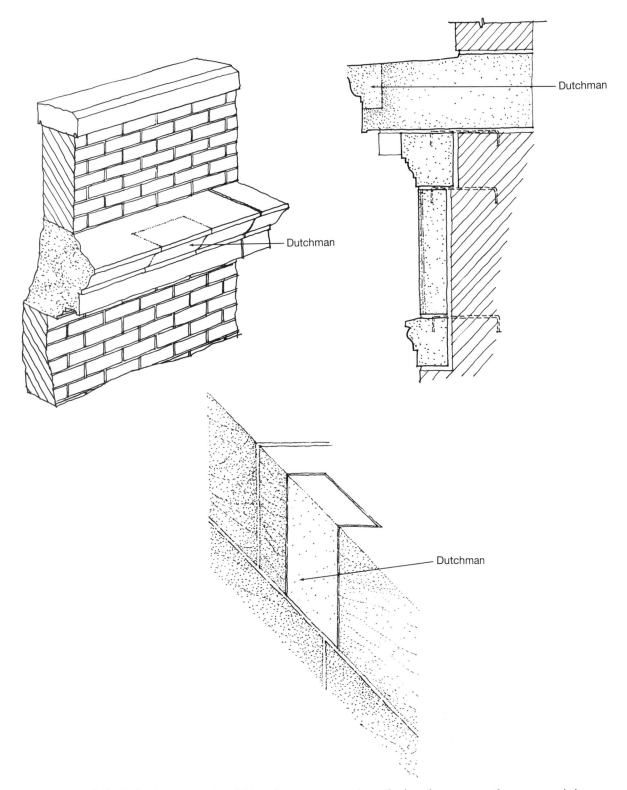

FIGURE 3.5. *A dutchman, or pieced-in replacement stone, is used where large areas of stone are missing.*

men, these should be anchored with cramps or dowels as well as adhesive. Care must be taken to ensure that the characteristics of the adhesive are compatible with the stone. Some adhesives do not expand and contract sufficiently.

Adhering Cracks. In some instances, the integrity of cracked stone blocks can be reestablished by injecting an adhesive into the cracks without removing the blocks. Before this procedure is performed, it should be determined that the crack is no longer active and that the forces that created the crack will not cause the stone to crack again. After cleaning out the crack and placing a temporary seal on the surface, structural adhesive is introduced into the cracks through injection ports.

Anchored Composite Patches. In some instances, stone surfaces are so badly decayed that composite repairs must be anchored. In these cases, noncorrosive anchoring pins should be inserted into the original stone in addition to the holes that anchor the stone patch. Although stainless steel pins are commonly used, threaded teflon pins eliminate the problem of condensation around the "cold spots" introduced by metal pins.

Reusing Existing Stone Blocks. If deterioration has progressed too far for surface retooling but not so far that the structural integrity of the blocks has been lost, it is sometimes possible to remove the stone blocks and to provide a new finished surface. This new surface can be on either the front or rear face of the stone. When major portions of the blocks are removed, the remaining pieces will require a cast stone backup to provide a block of proper depth for the opening. Alternately, the space behind the thinned facing may be filled with brick masonry.

New Stone Blocks. When deterioration has progressed to the point that individual blocks of stone have to be replaced, new stone blocks can be provided. (Fig. 3.6) The new stone should match the original stone in color, graining, finish, and light reflectance, as well as in physical and chemical properties.

Structural Repair

All remedial work on a stone masonry façade that has structural consequences and thus affects the stability of the wall should be designed and supervised by a professional with experience in similar work.

In all repair procedures, new anchors, ties, dowels, or rods should be of noncorrosive metal or plastic. Materials that have been used include stainless steel, titanium, nylon, teflon, and delrin. Whatever the material, care should be taken so that the thermal coefficients of the stone and of the anchors are as close as possible, or so that the design of the system allows for any differences. Those supports that are tied into a skeletal system should be attached so that no galvanic action can occur at the point of contact.

FIGURE 3.6. *New stone units can be used when restoration and repair are not possible. New stone should match the original in physical, chemical, and aesthetic properties.* Raymond M. Pepi, President, Building Conservation Associates, Inc.

When incompatible materials are used, galvanic corrosion can cause the supports to deteriorate until they fail.

CLEANING STONE MASONRY

Of the several reasons for cleaning masonry façades, the desire for aesthetic improvement is usually the chief motivation. More important, however, cleaning can help to stabilize deterioration processes when the soiling present is detrimental to masonry materials. In addition, removal of heavy soiling is vital to accurately diagnosing surface conditions. Cleaning is also an essential step in preparing the masonry surface for the application of paints and coatings.

The goal of any cleaning project is to clean the masonry using a method that does no damage, or, at most, minimal damage, to the masonry substrate while achieving the desired results. With historic structures, cleaning should restore the original appearance of the masonry; overcleaning should be avoided. Selection of the most appropriate cleaning materials and techniques for the project depends on the nature of the substrate to be cleaned as well as on the composition of the soiling present.

Precleaning Processes

Evaluation of Substrate and Soiling. The first step in designing an effective cleaning program is to identify the substrate to be cleaned. Ideally, a geologist or conservator should visit the building to examine the masonry. On projects where time and budget constraints make a visit impossible, the masonry should be identified through building records or laboratory testing.

Before a cleaning method can be selected, the soiling must be characterized. Most soiling consists of foreign matter such as soot, grease, biological growth, and graffiti, although alteration products such as weathering crusts and some metallic staining are also considered soiling. When soiling is a symptom of an ongoing deterioration process, the condition should be stabilized before cleaning is undertaken.

Laboratory Testing. Laboratory testing may be used to augment the information gained during the on-site survey. Samples removed from areas having representative conditions can be tested to determine their physical and chemical properties and further characterize the soiling present. For example, evaluation of water absorption characteristics aids in understanding staining mechanisms and deterioration patterns. Laboratory tests can be helpful in ruling out the use of potentially damaging cleaning methods and the identification of soluble salts can aid in determining the source of deterioration affecting the substrates.

Field Testing. Field testing provides the opportunity to evaluate the procedures, equipment, and necessary protective measures best suited for the particular project. Tests should be conducted to select the gentlest means possible. Cleaned areas should be evaluated over time so that long-range effects are known. Field testing is important in preventing the disappointment that often stems from unrealistic expectations of what cleaning can accomplish. On-site testing determines the effectiveness of the most promising cleaning systems under actual field conditions.

Specifications and Supervision. Laboratory and field testing facilitate selection of an appropriate cleaning method and help to identify the measures that will be required for worker safety and for protecting adjacent materials. Once the cleaning method has been selected, clear, concise specifications should be developed for the project to ensure that the work is carried out in the most effective way. Inspection of the project while in progress should be undertaken to ensure that all products and processes are implemented as specified.

Methods Used in Cleaning Stone Masonry

The cleaning method selected should remove the soiling without adversely affecting the mineralogical composition of the masonry material or its surface texture. Methods that have been employed to clean masonry building façades include the use of water washing, chemical cleaning, and abrasive cleaning.

Water Washing. The cleaning method thought to be the simplest and safest is washing with water. Water washing is a versatile cleaning method; aqueous techniques include spraying and misting, pressure washing, and steam cleaning.

With some types of soiling, contact with water softens the deposit, enabling its removal. In other cases, water is actually a solvent for the soiling. Sometimes, the addition of a detergent to the spray or mist helps to loosen and dissolve dirt. The effectiveness of water washing calcareous substrates such as limestone and marble relies on the fact that soiling is often trapped in the weathering crust that has formed on the surface. The crust is slightly water soluble, and washing with water loosens both the crust and the soiling material trapped within.

Equipment for spraying and misting can be as simple as perforated hoses or sprinkler heads that direct water to the soiled area for an extended period. The spray or mist can be continuous or intermittent with alternating on and off wash cycles. Scrubbing is sometimes used to facilitate removal of the loosened material. With pressure washing, the minimum effective water pressure required to remove soiling is used, avoiding excessive pressures that might erode or abrade the masonry. Steam cleaning requires more sophisticated equipment and presents additional safety concerns for operators. Although steam cleaning has been effective in removing certain types of soiling, it is not widely used for cleaning masonry façades.

Water washing methods also have limitations. Prolonged contact with water can induce mineralogical changes that produce staining. Water damage to interior materials, corrosion of embedded ferrous metals, and subsequent freeze/thaw damage to the façade are always concerns. Regarding the latter, cleaning should never be scheduled in cold weather months. Water washing can also be time-consuming and has limited effectiveness in removing many types of soiling.

Chemical Cleaning. When water washing is not effective in removing soiling, chemical cleaning is sometimes used. There are a variety of chemical cleaning products from which to chose. Detergents—which can be used in conjunction with water washing—often provide the gentlest cleaning. With nonionic detergents, there is no danger of salt formation and efflorescence; however, water rinsing should follow cleaning to remove detergent residues that attract soiling. Acidic cleaners contain dilute mineral acids such as hydrochloric, hydrofluoric, phosphoric and/or organic acids such as acetic and citric. They are used to remove heavy soiling from building stones such as sandstone and unpolished granite, which are not sensitive to acids. Care has to be taken, however, to avoid damaging the mortar, which can be dissolved by acids. The cleaning process involves applying the diluted cleaner to the prewetted surface and allowing a short dwell period. Residual cleaning chemical and soiling residues are removed by pressure water rinsing. (Fig. 3.7)

Alkaline cleaners based on sodium or potassium hydroxide are used to clean heavily soiled acid-sensitive materials such as limestone and marble. Alkaline cleaners soften or

FIGURE 3.7. *Water washing can be a very effective cleaning technique for certain types of stone; when water washing does not work, chemical cleaning is used.* Ricardo Viera, Senior Conservator, Building Conservation Associates, Inc.

break down encrusted soiling deposits, enabling removal with water rinsing. A neutralizing acidic cleaner must be applied to remove any latent traces of alkali and complete the cleaning operation. A final water rinse thoroughly flushes the surfaces free of all cleaning residues. Sometimes, alkaline cleaners are used to clean heavy soiling on brick or sandstone. Depending on the severity of soiling, the cleaner can be applied either generally to the surface or selectively to areas of concentrated soiling.

Formulations with reduced acid and alkali contents are especially appropriate for cleaning historic masonry façades. These products also minimize problems associated with containment or collection of effluent because low-volume water rinsing is possible. Cleaners formulated with a thickened or gel-like consistency that minimize dripping and spillage are also useful in many instances.

The inappropriate or indiscriminate use of chemical cleaning can result in irreversible damage to the substrate. Because of this potential for damage, identification of the masonry material is imperative. During chemical cleaning, precautions must be taken to protect workers from exposure to potential health hazards.

Acidic cleaners should not be applied to acid-sensitive substrates of historic structures. Excessive concentrations and extended dwell periods produce etching, erosion, and staining. With alkaline cleaners, efflorescence can be caused by inadequate rinsing or failure to neutralize the surface.

Poultices are often useful to remove staining that has permeated the masonry surface. A poultice combines a dry, absorbent powder with a liquid to form a wet paste. The liquid can be water or a detergent or other chemical solution. When the poultice is applied to the surface, the liquid reacts with the surface and subsurface soiling during an extended dwell period. Solubilized soiling is drawn out into the absorbent powder and removed from the surface with the poultice. Cleaning proceeds in a controlled fashion and rinsing requirements are minimized.

Abrasive Cleaning. Abrasive cleaning involves scraping, grinding, or blasting the masonry surface with a dry or wet medium to mechanically remove soiling. Traditional abrasive cleaning methods, which clean by eroding the surface, are generally harsher than water and chemical cleaning and are not recommended for historic façades. In the past several years, however, several innovative abrasive techniques have emerged that may be more appropriate for cleaning masonry of historic structures.

Soda blasting, originally developed to clean the copper cladding of the Statue of Liberty, consists of blasting with bicarbonate of soda and water. The technique has been used to remove graffiti from masonry façades. However, because improper use of this technique has resulted in irreversible damage to masonry, soda blasting remains controversial.

Another new abrasive cleaning technique is blasting with pelletized carbon dioxide. This technique is similar to traditional abrasive cleaning except that a temperature of minus 73 degrees centigrade is maintained throughout the cleaning process. On impact, the pellets create a thermal differential or "shock" between the soil and the masonry surface. As the carbon dioxide pellets expand, soiling is loosened and flushed away. Because the carbon dioxide dissipates, disposal of cleaning effluent is simplified.

"Façade gommage," another abrasive cleaning method, was developed in France and involves the use of fine glass particles that are blown at the surface at a very low pressure. The particles rub parallel on the surface rather than striking it directly. Tests have shown that the method can be very gentle when used on some stone surfaces. Because the technique is proprietary and can only be performed by the technicians of the company that developed it, quality control is greater than what is normally possible with traditional abrasive techniques. During the cleaning process, the dust is collected in a vacuum chamber attached to the scaffolding from which the cleaning is done.

The Jos cleaning process, another new abrasive cleaning process, uses a mixture of low air pressure, a fine abrasive powder, and very little water (1.5 to 12 gallons per hour) which is delivered to the surface using special equipment. The Jos nozzle produces a rotating vortex, which removes general soiling as well as graffiti and paint from masonry surfaces. Although these new techniques are promising, there are always limitations to consider with abrasive cleaning processes. An important concern is preventing the abrasive material from damaging the surface as the dirt is removed. Abrasive cleaning can roughen stone surfaces, dull arrises, remove detail from stone carvings, and loosen or remove mortar. It can also etch unprotected metal and glass surfaces. With traditional abrasive cleaning systems, a great deal of airborne dust is usually generated.

Safety and Environmental Considerations

Planning for any cleaning project should include consideration of the effluent that will be produced. Any waste is considered hazardous if it causes injury or death, or damages or pollutes air, land, or water. Sources of hazardous waste from cleaning operations include effluent with a high or low pH, some spent organic solvents, and lead paint solids. Although hazardous waste is more often a concern with chemical cleaning operations, disposal of effluent from water washing and abrasive cleaning may also be governed by federal, state, or local regulations.

Specifications for stone masonry cleaning should require that all measures necessary to protect the health and safety of those involved in the work and of the general public and to protect the environment from damage are provided by the contractor.

NOTES

1. C.A. Grissom, "Deterioration and Treatment of Volcanic Stone: a review of the literature," in *Lavas and Volcanic Tuffs* edited by A. Elena Charola, Robert J. Koestler, and Gianni Lombardi, (Roma, 1994), 4.

2. R.J. Schaffer, *The Weathering of Natural Building Stones* (London, 1932, reprinted 1972), 7.

3. G.G. Amoroso and V. Fassina, *Stone Decay and Conservation* (Amsterdam, 1983), 2.

4. M.E. Hale, *The Biology of Lichens*, 3rd ed. (London, 1983), 2.

5. It is not known whether these materials were applied as protective or consolidating treatments. Oil and wax treatments were still in use in the 20th century when both were used extensively for Egyptian limestone sculpture at the Metropolitan Museum of Art in New York.

6. It is not exactly true to say that alkoxysilane treatments were born in the 1960s. As early as 1861, tetraethoxysilane (a.k.a. TEOS or ethyl silicate) was suggested by von Hoffman as a treatment for the deteriorating Clipsham limestone at the Houses of Parliment in London. The art technologist A.P. Laurie conducted extensive testing with the material in the 1920s. However, it was not until the development of WACKER OH—a catalyzed system also based on TEOS—that these materials were applied with regularity. Also at this time, researchers and conservators in England, including Hempel, Moncrieff, Larson, Arnold, and Price, developed stone consolidants based on methyltrimethoxysilane (MTMOS). In addition, water glass has been used since the 19th century and is chemically similar to alkoxysilanes because silicon-oxygen-silicon bonds are the primary linkages. The system is stabilized by alkali metals such as sodium and potassium, the residues of which, after the solidification of the silicates, are prone to carbonation by atmospheric carbon dioxide. The sodium and potassium carbonate salts can later cause deterioration of the stone, and, for this reason, water glass fell out of favor as a stone consolidant.

7. Seymour Lewin of New York University developed this system. Lewin's system involves the precipitation of barium carbonate which, in settings where sulfuric acid rain or sulfur dioxide gas are present, converts to barium sulfate. The barium hydroxide-urea treatment currently is not often used.

8. Acrylic resins are generally more stable to solar UV than most other organic resins. Rohm and Haas's B72 acrylic resin is an excellent example, which accounts for its widespread use as an art conservation material. Selwitz has pointed out that advances have also been made in the creation of more stable epoxy resin systems.

9. In addition to flammability, stricter laws concerning volatile organic compounds may limit the use of consolidation systems in the future.

4

BRICK MASONRY

Contributions by Frances Gale

THE ELEMENTS OF BRICK masonry are bricks and mortar. The properties of these materials, the ways in which the bricks are interlocked (the bond), and, if the masonry is not self-supporting, the method by which the masonry is supported are the factors determining the performance of a brick masonry façade. Mortar, as a material that is also used in other masonry construction with stone, terra-cotta, and cast stone, is discussed in Chapter 7.

HISTORICAL BACKGROUND

Baked clay units laid in mortar have been used as a building material for thousands of years. Bricks have been manufactured wherever the right ingredients and fuel were available. The Romans built immense brick masonry structures both in Italy and as far away as Britain, and brick construction persisted through medieval times. Craftspeople from the brickmaking centers of the Low Countries migrated to England and took their building practices with them. The strong brickworking tradition of the Low Countries also made its way to the British colonies in America. The Dutch erected brick buildings of excellent craftsmanship in New Amsterdam and in their settlements in the Hudson Valley. Even in many houses of wood, the most prevalent building material, brick masonry was used for chimneys and foundations. At first, bricks were often manufactured at individual building sites, but brickyards were eventually established near most communities.

Most brick masonry walls built before the development of the iron and steel skeletal frame in the 19th century were bearing walls, which supported not only their own weight but also portions of the buildings' floor and roof loads. In standard attached structures in large cities, however, the front and rear exterior walls typically supported only themselves, as the building loads were supported on the party or side walls. As building heights increased, the walls became thicker to support greater weights. These thick, multiple-wythe brick walls usually had a skin of face brick with lower-quality common brick as infill material.

The masonry above windows, doors, and other openings in brick walls was supported either by brick arches (round or flat) or by a lintel of continuous homogeneous material, preferably one with a relatively high tensile strength. In early construction, lintels were of wood; later, they were generally of iron or steel, although wooden lintels were still being used in the first quarter of the 20th century. Historically, stone lintels were also used to span openings in brick masonry. Stone, however, does not have the tensile strength of other materials and has been known to fail from faults not apparent at the time of construction.

The development of cast-iron and, later, steel skeletal frames eliminated the need for heavy, load-bearing walls, but sturdy, fire-resistant brick masonry was still a natural choice for a facing material. The masonry was supported from the metal skeleton by iron or steel lintels. Solid brickwork gave way to the cavity wall to help keep water from the interior of the building. Countless thousands of buildings across the United States have brick masonry skins supported by metal frames.

In the 1950s, glazed brick with a fired silica coating came into wide use since it came in an almost limitless variety of colors and had a sleek appearance much admired at the time. The material continued to be used extensively until recently. Its use in northern climates has fallen sharply because of the severe deterioration caused by forces exerted by the freezing and thawing of water trapped behind the glaze in many installations.

Because bricks, as small rectangular elements, did not lend themselves to many forms of traditional ornament, large-scale ornament on brick façades was often of stone or terracotta. Sometimes bricks were molded in special shapes or were rubbed or gauged after manufacture to provide ornamental details. Several forms of ornament used bricks in their natural shape in geometrical patterns where the bricks either projected slightly from the plane of the wall or were recessed slightly behind it. Corbeling was a form of ornamentation—used mainly for string courses and for cornices—in which each successive row of bricks projected over the one below it. It was possible for brick ornament to project a considerable distance in this manner as long as the weight of the masonry above the projecting brickwork provided a sufficient force to resist its bending moment. (Fig. 4.1)

MANUFACTURING PROCESS

From its beginning, the brickmaking process has consisted of the same basic steps—obtaining and tempering the clay, and molding, drying, and burning the bricks—which have been developed and automated over time. Clay, a fine-grained material of particles eroded from rocks and deposited along the banks of waterways, is collected from natural deposits and broken up to increase its consistency and plasticity. The clay is mixed with

FIGURE 4.1. *Brick is used for various façade elements and forms of ornament such as arches, string courses, cornices, and pediments.* James V. Banta, New York Landmarks Conservancy

sand or other tempering material, to provide stability and reduce shrinkage, and with water, to provide a consistency suitable for forming. The mixture is shaped into bricks, and the bricks are dried and fired.

In early times, clay was often dug, spread on the ground, and left to weather over the winter so that alternating freezing and thawing would break it up. Depending on the characteristics of the clay, it was mixed with sand or other tempering material and water by hand or with simple animal-powered machinery. A lump of the tempered clay was thrown into a wooden mold, the surface was struck off, and the wet brick was removed from the mold and dried in the sun.

After drying, the bricks were stacked to form a clamp or kiln. The bricks on the inside of the kiln were spaced to allow heat to reach all sides; those on the outside were placed next to each other and the outside surface was plastered to contain the heat. Fuel stacked in the center of the kiln was ignited, and the bricks were fired. In early kilns, the heat at the center was greater than that at the edges, and the bricks near the center were burned harder than the others. Although bricks can be obtained from similar kilns today, more evenly burned bricks have been available for almost 150 years.

During the mid-19th century, the brickmaking process became more controlled. Natural clays were ground and processed to eliminate pebbles and to improve consistency; later, during the second half of the century, shales and similar types of rocks were ground by machine to provide an even more uniform material. Machines were invented to work and mix the clay and to shape the bricks, which were generally formed either by being pressed into a mold or by being cut from a continuous mass of clay extruded through dies. It also became possible to more closely control the temperature of the kiln. Still later, the development of continuous tunnel kilns in which wheeled platforms stacked with bricks moved slowly through tunnels, which were warm at each end and hot in the center, allowed the firing process to be precisely controlled. All of these changes affected the qualities of the bricks, leading to a harder, denser, and more uniform product. Even so, bricks made from different clays or formed by different methods can have widely varying properties.

PROPERTIES

The properties of bricks depend on the many variables in the manufacturing process, including the composition of the clay, the temper, the method by which they are formed, and the conditions under which they are fired. These variables can cause differences even in bricks manufactured in the same place and time, and bricks across the centuries can vary considerably.

There are many kinds of clay, the basic ingredient in bricks, with different compositions and origins. Pure clays are basically hydrous aluminum silicates with small quantities of other substances such as oxides of iron, lime, magnesium, and alumina. These impurities in the clays give bricks different colors when they are fired: ferric oxide produces a characteristic red color, lime produces yellow or greenish-yellow bricks, and magnesia and alumina produce buff-colored bricks.

Because the way bricks are made has changed greatly over the years, the properties of modern bricks are often quite different from those of bricks used in earlier centuries. Early bricks made of clay mixed on the ground and thrown into molds by hand can contain pebbles and air pockets and can be of uneven density. Bricks made of clay mixed in mechanical pug mills and extruded through dies are generally more consistant, and bricks pressed in steel molds under high pressure are denser and stronger still. As manufacturing processes became more sophisticated, the ingredients and consistency of the mix also became more controlled.

More controlled firing, allowing more even heating of the bricks, also produced more uniform, higher-quality bricks. During firing, porosity is reduced, and a physical bond is developed between the particles by partial fusion and/or sintering of the amorphous constituents.

The properties that make bricks valuable for the construction of exterior walls include their compressive strength and fire and weather resistance. The physical quality of brick masonry is also controlled by the properties of bricks that affect their ability to bond with mortar, including surface pore structure, initial rate of absorption, and tensile strength.

Properties of bricks that affect the visual character of the wall include size, color, and surface texture. Surfaces reflect the method of forming; they can be sand-struck, water-struck, wire-cut, or pressed. The faces can be coated with a pigmented silica glaze to provide a smooth, glossy surface in colors not found in natural clays.

Two types of bricks have traditionally been used in building exterior walls: face bricks and common bricks. Face bricks are used in the outer face of the wall because they are harder, more regular, and more uniform than common bricks. They are better able to resist weathering and give a more attractive appearance. Common bricks are used for inner wythes of the wall and often for side and rear walls not visible from the front of the building.

USE OF BRICK MASONRY IN BUILDING FAÇADES

Brick masonry walls are formed by interlocking bricks and filling the spaces or joints between them with mortar. In addition to being the adhesive that holds the bricks together, the mortar also prevents water from entering the wall, evens out the heights or levels of the brick courses, and distributes the weight evenly between the courses. The mortar joints between the bricks vary in width from the minimum effective dimension of about 3/16-inch to 1/2-inch depending on the type of brick used and the style of the building. Different joint profiles are discussed in Chapter 7, Mortar.

Where brick masonry is used for bearing walls, the bricks, because they are so small, must be laid at least two rows, or wythes, thick and sometimes several more depending on the height of the wall and the load it must carry. These rows of brick must be joined together to function as a unit. The configurations in which the bricks are interlocked to secure the wythes together is called the bond. (Fig. 4.2) Most brick masonry bonds consist of a combination of stretchers, which give walls strength in the longitudinal direction, and headers, which give walls strength in the transverse direction. (Fig. 4.3) Wythes of brickwork consisting of all stretchers can be united by metal ties or metal-trussed reinforcement.

In buildings with iron and steel frames, brick masonry serves as an enclosing skin but does not support the weight of the building's loads or even its own weight for more than one or two stories. The brickwork is supported from the metal skeleton by iron or steel lintels or relieving angles. Early brick masonry used in this manner was solid brick or

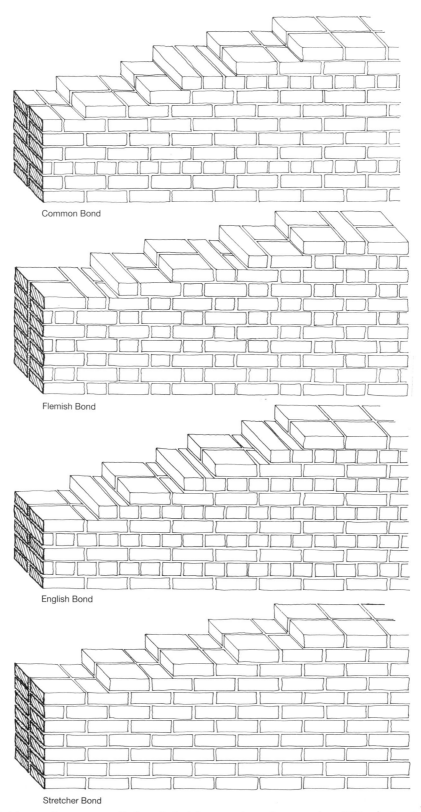

Common Bond

Flemish Bond

English Bond

Stretcher Bond

FIGURE 4.2. *Bricks can be structurally interlocked in a variety of ways using different bond patterns, which also create different decorative appearances.*

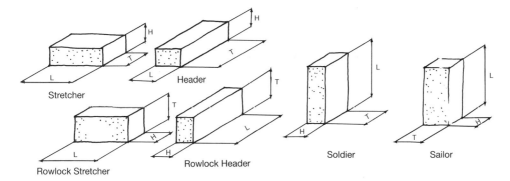

FIGURE 4.3. *Brick faces are identified in different ways depending on their orientation.*

brick backed by clay tile. Later, the cavity wall was developed to help prevent water and moisture from reaching the interior of the structure. In cavity walls, the two wythes of masonry, the face brick, and the backup material, are separated by a space or cavity and tied together with either brick, tile, or metal ties. The back of the exterior wythe was often parged with mortar to help exclude water. After problems developed when water accumulated inside early cavity walls, new features (such as flashing and weepholes over lintels and relieving angles) were introduced to direct any water that penetrated the outer layer back to the exterior surface.

DETERIORATION AND EVALUATION OF BRICK MASONRY

A careful examination of the brick masonry portions of the façade should expose any problems with the masonry or its support. The simplest form of brick deterioration is surface erosion, where only the surface is damaged. Joint failure of any kind, cracked bricks, bricks whose surface is spalling, and missing bricks indicate more serious problems. Deteriorated anchors or reinforcements may be more serious still, indicating possible instability of the masonry. Failure of the supporting structural members, is the most serious since the structural stability of the façade is threatened.

The masonry should be inspected for open joints, cracks, bulges, and other displacements. The locations of anchors and reinforcement can usually be determined with a metal detector. If the causes of failure are not visibly apparent, probes to determine support conditions and tests to determine stresses in the masonry may be required.

Deterioration Related to the Properties of Brick

Several causes of brick masonry deterioration derive from the characteristics of the brick itself. Old bricks, made before careful quality control of clay mixtures and firing temperatures, frequently develop cracks where shrinkage and laminating occurred in the clay or where unequal stresses were set up during firing. Early bricks prepared by the hand-molding process were less dense and more porous than later extruded or machine-pressed bricks. They can absorb between 20 and 25 percent of their weight in water and are thus especially susceptible to the action of freeze/thaw cycles. By the end of the 19th century, the accepted maximum water absorption was 10 percent or less. Bricks, like other clay products, may increase in size slightly as they absorb water. This expansion, which is not completely reversible as the material dries out, can cause stresses in the wall.

Deterioration Related to Improper Details, Specifications, and Workmanship

Many causes of masonry failure can be traced to improper details, specifications, and workmanship. Among these are the causes of failure related to the failure to keep water out of the wall and to properly design systems of supports and anchors. There are numerous additional causes.

Failure of brick masonry may occur because individual bricks and mortar were not properly bonded into a cohesive unit. When the method of bonding is insufficient or when it fails, the strength of the wall is impaired. If movement occurs because of this failure, cracks may open and further deterioration occurs. Bond failure may result from a bond pattern that did not sufficiently reinforce the wall in either the longitudinal or transverse direction, or from a lack of adhesion between the mortar and the bricks.

The major bonding mechanism between bricks and mortar is mechanical. The mortar paste enters the brick's surface pores and sets. These pores should be of sufficient size to allow penetration and should provide undercuts, such as that given by a spherical opening with a narrow neck, to assist adhesion. Glassy bricks with no surface pores will develop a bond strength that is much less than that of bricks of the same composition with open surface pores.

If the bricks were frozen or completely saturated when they were laid, the original strength of the bond between the mortar and the brick may be poor or nonexistent because the brick was unable to absorb any water (its initial rate of absorption was zero) and thus to draw mortar paste into its pores. While the capillarity of the brick should be sufficient to pull mortar paste into the brick's pores, it should not be high enough to remove the water from the mortar before the mortar can penetrate the pores.

It is also possible that the mortar joints were not properly made; that is, mortar may not have been applied over the full surface of the brick. If mortar was applied only near the edges, the joints may be weak and susceptible to water penetration. Or the head joints may not have been shoved full; too often, head joints were slushed full, leading to voids and weak mortar. Even small cracks where mortar failed to adhere to a brick may allow water to enter and accelerate deterioration.

Failure may also occur because the brick and mortar are not suited to each other. The use of portland cement has produced mortars of higher compressive strength but lower water retentivity and workability than earlier lime-sand mortars. Consequently, the development of a good bond between the brick and mortar has become more difficult and more demanding on the properties of the brick. Thus, the use of a modern mortar with an old brick may be inappropriate. In addition, there has been a recent trend toward the use of air-entraining agents to improve mortar workability. These additives increase the porosity and permeability of the mortar, and reduce its compressive strength.

Until failures led to the study of large unbroken expanses of brick masonry, whole walls—indeed, whole building exteriors—were often constructed without soft joints to relieve stresses produced by expansion of the bricks caused by water absorption and expansion and contraction caused by variations in temperature.

Where brick masonry was used as an exterior cladding supported on the building's structural system, failure may have occurred because of inadequate support, anchoring, or provisions for relieving stress. Supports may not have been protected sufficiently from water. Corroded iron or steel anchors may have expanded sufficiently to crack the wall. Anchors were often not installed as frequently as they should have been; or, if the anchors were installed where required, it is possible that they have deteriorated. The cumulative weight of an inadequately anchored wall may cause areas of the masonry to buckle outward. It is also possible that the original construction did not provide sufficient provisions for movement of the masonry elements—a requirement especially important in multistory structures. Where brick masonry was too rigidly connected to the metal supporting structure, substantial vertical cracking may have occurred to relieve the stresses caused by thermal movement or water absorption. This cracking accelerates weathering and deterioration. Once either the brick itself cracked or the mortar joints between the pieces failed, water was free to enter, and corrosion of the ferrous metal anchors may have begun.

Steel, concrete, and brick masonry all have different thermal coefficients: they change dimensions at different rates with fluctuating temperatures. These different dimensional changes may have led to the cracking of a masonry wall if differential movements caused by variations in temperature were restrained by an inflexible anchoring system or by the lack of expansion joints or inadequate expansion joints. Symptoms of this condition are patterned cracks appearing at corners, piers, or other locations where the mass of the wall changes. (Fig. 4.4)

Cracking may have been caused by settlement resulting from improper foundations or from out-of-level or -plumb construction. Inadequate detailing of the structure may have led to other damage of masonry walls. If adequate flashing at the roof line and other systems to convey water away from the wall were not provided, serious damage may have occurred.

Deterioration Related to Effects of Exposure and Use

Brick saturated with water and subsequently exposed to freezing temperatures may be destroyed by the force created by the expansion of the water as it freezes. The appear-

FIGURE 4.4. *Cracks on the corner of a brick building may indicate the failure of brickwork caused by differential expansion and contraction between the brick masonry and steel framing.* James V. Banta, New York Landmarks Conservancy

ance of failure is normally a crumbling or disintegration of the unit or a delamination of the face. Although most bricks can withstand freezing and thawing without damage, units with inadequate properties will show signs of damage from those forces. Water absorption in excess of 12 percent suggests susceptibility to deterioration by freeze/thaw mechanisms.

Although properly fired brick has unusual resistance to chemical attack under normal atmospheric conditions, inadequately fired units are subject to such attack. Sulfuric acid solution developed from atmospheric conditions will dissolve the brick at a rate approximately ten times higher than it will be dissolved by pure water. However, the resulting salts are more damaging to the appearance of the building than to its actual strength, leaving staining and efflorescence on the masonry structure. The sulfur trioxide required for this attack may come from pollutants in the atmosphere, but it can also come from the masonry units themselves. Units produced in a high sulfur atmosphere may contain residual sulfates, which will become acidic in the presence of water. The cement constituents of mortars may contain high quantities of sulfates and alkalis as well, and solutions of these constituents may accelerate attack of the brick.

FIGURE 4.5. *Subflorescence, or the crystallization of soluble salts in the pores of brick, can cause the deterioration similar to that of freeze/thaw cycles, resulting in a spalled brick surface.* James V. Banta, New York Landmarks Conservancy

Moisture in a wall from rising damp, rainwater, and condensation may carry acids, which attack the bricks and mortar. The water may also carry soluble salts that subfloresce, or crystallize, in the pores of a brick, causing failure similar to that produced by freeze/thaw cycles. With repeated wetting and temperature cycling, crystallized salts will produce an expansive force sufficient to disintegrate the unit. (Fig. 4.5) Moisture in the wall may cause corrosion of ferrous anchors. Acids in the water may also adversely affect the anchors.

Bricks will exhibit some expansion when exposed to moisture, especially when they are underfired. Although this moisture expansion is usually minor (about 0.04 percent), the presence of particles of lime or gypsum in the clay can cause still higher moisture expansion—an expansion great enough to destroy walls. Reactions between the fired clay and alkali solutions from the mortar or other sources may also result in large expansions.

Airborne particles may damage the exterior surface of the bricks over time by abrading the hard surface and exposing the softer interior. Uneven settlement caused by changes in the subsurface conditions or changes in loading may cause cracking in brick masonry. Finally, internal stresses in the masonry resulting from any of the causes discussed may cause the header bricks that bond wythes of brick masonry together to crack.

Deterioration Resulting from Improper Maintenance

Abrading a masonry surface by sandblasting or dissolving the surface with inappropriate chemical cleaners will expose more of the softer interior parts of the brick to the elements. The outer crust of a brick is harder and denser than the material inside. Once this crust is removed by surface spalling from moisture-related mechanisms, restricted expansion and contraction, sandblasting, or chemical etching, disentegration of the brick is greatly accelerated.

Application of water-vapor-impermeable coatings in the past may have led to damage of the brick. Coatings containing silicone or based on finely ground cement may have been applied with the intention of protecting the wall, but water entering the wall in some other location may have contained soluble salts or may have dissolved soluble salts from the masonry. The salt solution may then have migrated toward the barrier, and the salts may have crystallized behind it. This disruptive force may have broken the coated face away from the masonry unit. Damage could also have resulted from expansion of condensed water passing through freeze/thaw cycles. If a relatively vapor-impermeable coating was applied over an entire masonry wall and any water was able to enter, salt crystallization or freeze/thaw cycles could have caused severe damage to the masonry.

Face spalling in glazed brick usually results from similar circumstances. Spalling is an inherent and irremediable defect of this material when it is used in northern climates.

The problems with this material may be worse if moisture enters the mortar joints and migrates into the brick. Because the moisture is trapped behind the glazed face, the unit is subject to all of the destructive forces caused by the presence of water in the pores of the brick, and the face of the brick may spall off.

REPAIR OF BRICK MASONRY

The most common and most important repair of brick walls is repair or repointing of the mortar joints, which is discussed in Chapter 7, Mortar. Although several other methods may be used to repair damaged brickwork, most damaged brick masonry is taken down and replaced. It is, of course, necessary to take the same measures to prevent waterflow and water entry as those required on stone façades.

Minor Repair

Surface Coatings. Surface coatings have been applied to brick walls almost as long as they have been built. Walls are coated for two basic reasons: to change their appearance and to protect them. Early coatings included whitewash or lime. Later, the surfaces were coated with paints of different vehicles and pigments. Many modern coatings have been developed and applied to masonry walls in the last thirty years.

Coatings used on brick masonry should not form vapor barriers. They also should not be used in an attempt to provide a water-resistant membrane on an unsound masonry wall. Repointing joints with missing or deteriorated mortar is the proper method of reestablishing the wall's surface continuity. If the masonry surface is too deteriorated to provide adequate protection against water penetration, it will not provide a firm, sound surface to which a coating can adhere. Any coating applied over an unsound surface will be subject to rapid deterioration.

The use of vapor-impermeable coatings on brick masonry will almost certainly create problems. A continuous, unbroken membrane must be established for the coating to be effective. If any moisture should enter the wall through openings in the membrane, or from other sources, it will be trapped behind the membrane. This trapped moisture may lead to all the standard problems associated with water in the wall. Thus, application of popular cementitious coatings or silicones is not recommended.

Paints, stains, and oils may be used on brick masonry if they are vapor-permeable, so thus enabling any water vapor that enters the wall to escape through them. Although special water-based paints that allow water vapor to pass have been developed for use on brick masonry, these treatments require continuing maintenance. While providing a uniform appearance, paint coatings may hide deterioration in the brickwork until it is eventually revealed by peeling paint.

Silicate paints, used on masonry surfaces for many years in Europe, are available in the United States, where they have been used for over 20 years. These paints, containing ethyl silicates, form a chemical bond with the masonry. They are said to be colorfast and to last as long as fifty years.

Major Repair

Consolidation. When the surface of the brick wall has deteriorated to the point that it is soft and friable, it can be consolidated in the same way that stone walls are consolidated. It is important to determine that the consolidant will be compatible with the brick and the mortar and will not create a vapor barrier. Tests should be conducted on samples of the materials of the wall before the work is done. Consolidation is a relatively expensive treatment seldom used on brick masonry.

Reversal. If the exterior surfaces of the brick are severely deteriorated, it is sometimes possible to reverse the bricks if their interior faces are capable of withstanding atmospheric conditions. Before reversing bricks, they should be tested for hardness, absorption, and saturation coefficient.

Pressure Grouting. Pressure grouting with structural adhesives is one method of repairing cracks in brick walls that are not cavity walls, but it is a sophisticated technique that requires close professional supervision. Grouting will restore structural integrity and prevent water entry. Before this work is performed, however, every attempt should be made to determine that no large voids or cavities exist inside the wall and that the crack does not stem from chronic attempts to relieve thermal or other stresses. After that determination has been made, a temporary seal is applied to the crack, and injection ports are inserted at regular intervals. Adhesive is then injected into the ports. The adhesive used is often a clear, two-component, compatible epoxy resin compound.

Supplemental Anchors. The many failures of masonry walls caused by the lack of bond between the outer wythes of brickwork and the backup masonry, resulting from omitted or failed ties, have led to the relatively recent development of several different kinds of anchors that can be inserted through the exterior face of the wall or through the interior face if it is accessible to tie the portions of the wall together. In one type of anchor, a stainless steel rod centered in a mesh fabric sleeve is inserted in a hole drilled through the layers of masonry to be tied together. When filled with cementitious grout, the sleeve expands and the grout oozes through the sleeve to bond the masonry. Another type of anchor uses a twisted metal strip that is screwed into a hole of slightly smaller diameter. Still other types of anchors employ epoxy resins to glue stainless steel rods in holes in the masonry. In all cases, holes drilled in exposed masonry must be plugged or filled to match the adjacent surface.

Removal and Replacement. Displaced masonry, such as face work that has bulges, should be taken down and the bricks relaid in their original positions after any support failures contributing to the bulging brickwork have been corrected. Replaced sections of masonry must be properly tied into backup masonry with headers or noncorrosive anchors and ties, and be properly toothed into existing adjacent masonry using whole units and matching the existing bond pattern.

Cleaning Cavity Walls. When the exterior wythe of brick in a cavity wall is excessively wet, it may be possible to alleviate the problem by cleaning out the weepholes that should exist above flashings. When the water problem is caused by partially filled or bridged cavities, it is sometimes possible to remove two or three courses of brick above the flashings at the bottom of the wall and above openings. Excess mortar can be cleaned from the cavity and the masonry replaced with proper weepholes.

Repair of Structural Supports. The most serious restoration involving brick masonry walls requires that the supporting structure be repaired or replaced. This work can range

FIGURE 4.6. *This brick façade is being cleaned using a standard chemical cleaning process.*
Bessie Ballentine, Conservator, Building Conservation Associates, Inc.

from the replacement of deteriorated ties and anchors fastening the brickwork to the structure to the replacement of structural elements themselves, either the lintels and relieving angles directly supporting the masonry or the supporting steel framework. Repair of structural supports almost always requires removal and replacement of portions of the masonry. Work at this level, which affects the structural stability of the building, should be undertaken only under the direction of an experienced professional.

CLEANING BRICK MASONRY

A full discussion of masonry cleaning, including evaluation of the substrate and soiling, on-site and laboratory testing, methods of cleaning, and safety precautions, is included in Chapter 3, Stone Masonry. The goal in cleaning brick masonry should be to clean the surface using a method that achieves the desired results without damage to the masonry substrate. Overcleaning should always be avoided.

Because traditional abrasive cleaning methods damage brick surfaces, and washing with pure water is usually ineffective in removing all but light soiling, brick masonry is generally cleaned with chemical solutions in conjunction with water rinsing. (Fig. 4.6) Because the surface of glazed brick can be damaged by acidic and alkaline cleaning solutions, detergent cleaning is often most appropriate. With unglazed brick, acidic cleaning solutions can be evaluated when detergent cleaning is ineffective.

Acidic cleaners containing dilute mineral acids such as hydrochloric, hydrofluoric, phosphoric and/or organic acids such as acetic and citric are used to remove heavy soiling from most brick masonry. The cleaning process involves applying the diluted cleaner to the prewetted surface and allowing a short dwell period. Chemical and soiling residues are removed by pressure water rinsing. Great care should be used to avoid damage to mortar, which can be attacked by acids. Sometimes, alkaline cleaners are used to remove heavy soiling on brick surfaces, but the type of chemical cleaner should be selected with care, then tested in small areas before it is used to clean walls. Certain chemicals cause staining of some types of bricks, and soft brick are particularly vulnerable to damage from aggressive cleaning methods.

Formulations with reduced acid and alkali contents are especially appropriate for cleaning historic brick masonry, and many products can be effective even at greater dilutions than recommended by the manufacturer.

The inappropriate or indiscriminate use of chemical cleaning can result in irreversible damage to the substrate. In addition, precautions must be taken to protect workers from exposure to potential health hazards caused by the chemicals, and to provide proper collection and disposal of the effluent.

5

TERRA-COTTA MASONRY

Contributions by Frances Gale

A DISCUSSION OF TERRA-COTTA masonry must include the terra-cotta units, the mortar or sealant filling the joints between them, and the method by which the terra-cotta is supported. Mortar, as a material that is also used in other masonry construction is discussed in Chapter 7, and sealants are discussed in Chapter 12.

HISTORICAL BACKGROUND

Architectural terra-cotta (literally "cooked earth" in Italian), a fired clay product closely related to brick but made of finer clays, is one of the oldest and most popular building materials known to humankind. Sun-dried and burnt clay building units are known to have been used by ancient civilizations, including the Assyrians, Egyptians, Greeks, and Romans. The Chinese developed glazed terra-cotta in the 4th and 3th centuries B.C. During the late Middle Ages and the Renaissance, terra-cotta was widely used for architectural ornament and relief sculpture, first in Italy and later in northern Europe. Following the Renaissance, the material was little used in Europe until it was revived in England around the middle of the 19th century.

In the decades following the revival of the use of terra-cotta for architectural decoration in Europe, the material also became an important component of American building exteriors. Chicago's Great Fire of 1871 provided an impetus for the large-scale use of terra-cotta. The city needed to erect new fire-resistant buildings as quickly and cheaply as possible. Terra-cotta was not only an inexpensive fire-resistant material for enclosing structural iron or steel framing, but, because it was molded or extruded rather than carved, it could be used to reproduce familiar forms of ornament much more quickly and economically than if the ornament was carved from stone in the traditional manner. From only one model made by a sculptor, craftspeople, who did not need to be artisans, could take molds and cast numerous pieces.

In addition to terra-cotta's cost advantages over traditional ornamental materials, its light weight kept shipping charges to a minimum, and it could be installed by masons familiar with brick and stone (the only specialized labor required to produce it being in the factory). Its use quickly spread to other parts of the country. The material was widely used in New York City beginning in the 1880s. (Fig. 5.1) Terra-cotta in the form of flat panels, often resembling ashlar masonry, was used to clad whole building façades. In the form of medallions and other ornamental inlays, it was used to enliven façades of brick or other materials. Its plasticity—the ease with which it could be shaped—made it an especially valuable material for such sculptural façade elements as cornices, friezes, sills, and lintels, as well as elements in greater relief or that were freestanding, such as balustrades and columns. When it was used as ornament, the material was called architectural terra-

FIGURE 5.1. *A noteworthy example of an early 20th-century terra-cotta-clad building in Prospect Park, Brooklyn, New York.* James V. Banta, New York Landmarks Conservancy

cotta to distinguish it from structural terra-cotta, which was employed in the construction of walls, partitions, floor arches, and fire-resistant enclosures for steel columns.

Architectural terra-cotta could duplicate any form of ornament, which meant it could be used in buildings of different architectural styles. Early unglazed architectural terra-cotta was most frequently used for decorative units in brick masonry in much the same way as stone trim had been used traditionally. Prior to 1877, the prevailing color of terra-cotta used in Chicago was grayish buff to simulate Joliet limestone, a popular building material. In New York and elsewhere, dark red or brown terra-cotta was frequently used in place of brownstone. In the early 20th century, when intensive chemical experimentation by the manufacturers of terra-cotta yielded both matte and shiny glazed surfaces in an almost infinite variety of high-quality colors, architects designed ornament specifically to exploit the material's many colors. They also created ornament, exemplified by the lush foliate forms of Louis Sullivan, that made the most of terra-cotta's fluid and plastic qualities.

In buildings before and after the turn of the century, the material was often used as a substitute for marble and limestone. It was also frequently used on the upper stories of tall buildings to match the stonework used on the ground stories. In general, terra-cotta enjoyed widespread popularity from the 1880s to the 1930s, a period of complex architectural ornamentation and elaborate color effects for which the material was exceptionally suitable.

MANUFACTURING PROCESS

Although through the years, changes reflecting different aesthetic movements occurred in the outer appearance of the material, the hollow form of the terra-cotta block remained basically the same. Most terra-cotta block was approximately 4 inches deep, with a wall thickness of about 1 to 1-1/4 inches. Large pieces had interior webs for reinforcement.

The process of molding architectural terra-cotta involves considerable handwork today, as it did in the past. From designer's sketches, the manufacturer prepares shop drawings. Artisans then sculpt clay models, which are made slightly larger than the final pieces to allow for shrinkage when the terra-cotta is fired. Plaster of Paris molds taken from these models are made to be disassembled to allow removal of the pressed clay body.

The terra-cotta body consists of a mixture of prepared weathered clays, with a high and consistent vitrification point, blended with ground burnt clay, or grog, which reduces warpage and shrinkage during firing. A uniform layer of this clay mixture is pressed into the molds by hand, and interior stiffening webs are built up in larger pieces. Once the clay has dried sufficiently to hold its shape and surface, it is removed from the mold for further drying. At this stage, the piece may be worked by hand if it is necessary to smooth surfaces, sharpen edges, or undercut portions of the design. When thoroughly dry, the clay body is coated with slip or glaze and fired.

Slip is a near-liquid combination of clay and water that is brushed on exposed surfaces of unglazed terra-cotta to provide a smooth finish. Glazed terra-cotta receives a coating including silica, which vitrifies during firing to provide the glasslike surface, and minerals, which determine the color.

The firing of high-grade terra-cotta requires a temperature of more than 2,000 degrees Fahrenheit. In the firing process, the constituents of clay sinter around particles of grog to form a semivitreous solid, which is less porous, and therefore less absorbent of free moisture, than common building stones.[1] If the material is glazed, the silica vitrifies to provide a smooth glassy surface fused to the terra-cotta body.

After the 1920s, when problems of glazing in terra-cotta became apparent, manufacturers altered the production process to produce terra-cotta of higher-quality material. They also fired it harder so that it was more impermeable to water. Well-made terra-cotta does not rely on a glaze for protection. The body of the piece can stand alone, and the glaze is primarily a form of decoration.

INSTALLATION OF TERRA-COTTA IN FAÇADES

Traditionally, in the simplest terra-cotta installation, the terra-cotta lintels, sills, or other decorative elements that did not project significantly from the plane of the wall were simply installed with mortar as similar elements of stone trim would have been. The open backs of the blocks allowed them to be keyed into the backup masonry.

With larger elements and elements projecting from the plane of the façade, such as entablatures, terra-cotta blocks were set and mechanically anchored in place. Flat or simply profiled blocks of terra-cotta were usually anchored to the masonry backing with Z-shaped straps. (Fig. 5.2) Theoretically, each block was anchored individually with a strap anchor fitted into a recessed slot at the top, so that it would not interfere with the joint. Terra-cotta elements projecting only slightly from the plane of the wall, including small cornices and string courses, might be backfilled with mortar or brick, or fastened with bolts to resist the bending moment created. (Fig. 5.3) For larger overhanging horizontal elements, such as major cornices or balconies, different and sometimes elaborate support systems were necessary. Blocks were attached to angles or rods, or suspended from steel members used as outriggers with standard hook and dowel systems. (Fig. 5.4) When the system was properly designed, it allowed for some adjustment during installation.

Joints between the units, about 3/16-inch thick, were filled with a fine even mortar, taking care to ensure uniform pressure and loading. Jointing had to be designed so that required cutting or fitting would not injure the mouldings or ornamental units. For regular facing and ornamental details, lugs molded at the sides of the blocks could be ground individually during installation to achieve proper fit and spacing. This method provided sufficient adjustment to counteract the characteristic warping and irregular shrinkage of the terra-cotta units during firing and to allow proper alignment.

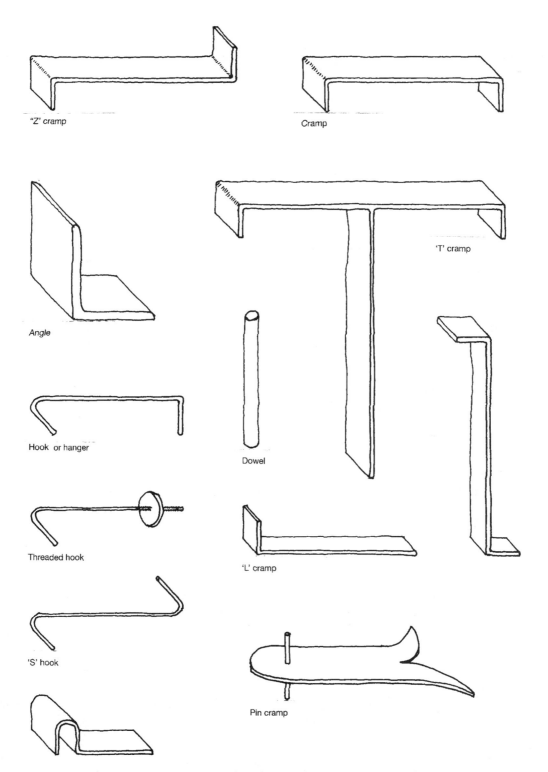

"Z" cramp

Cramp

Angle

'T' cramp

Hook or hanger

Dowel

Threaded hook

'L' cramp

'S' hook

Pin cramp

FIGURE 5.2. *Different cramps and anchors used in terra-cotta installation and repair.*

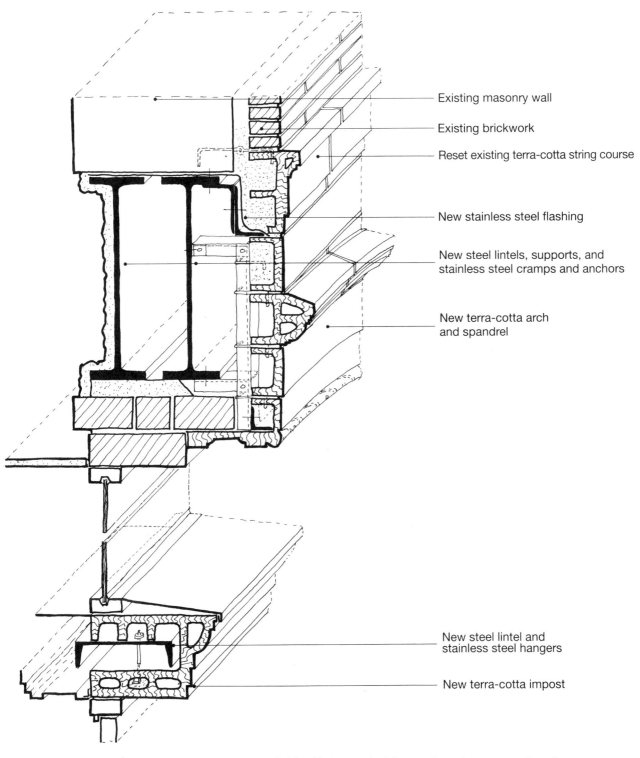

Existing masonry wall

Existing brickwork

Reset existing terra-cotta string course

New stainless steel flashing

New steel lintels, supports, and stainless steel cramps and anchors

New terra-cotta arch and spandrel

New steel lintel and stainless steel hangers

New terra-cotta impost

FIGURE 5.3. *Terra-cotta units are individually fastened with a variety of cramps and anchors.*

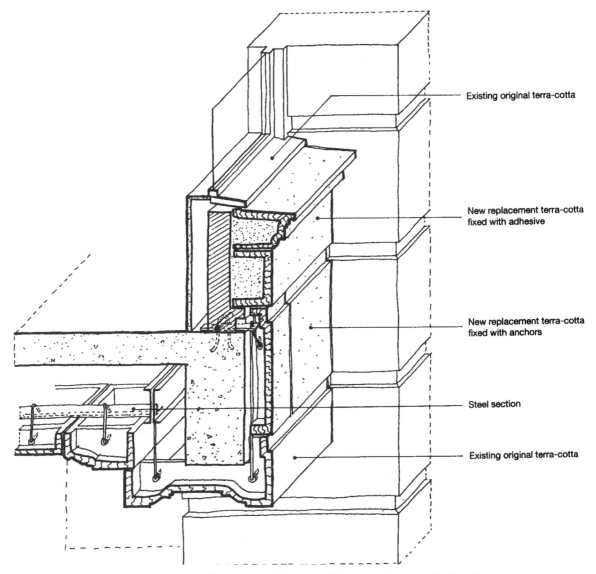

FIGURE 5.4. *Terra-cotta units can be supported from small steel sections attached to the building's structural frame.*

Frequently, hollow terra-cotta blocks were backfilled with brick masonry, mortar, or concrete, both to fireproof support members and to protect the anchoring systems from corrosion. It was important to provide backfill having the proper density and coefficient of expansion to prevent damage during cyclical changes in temperature. When the blocks were left hollow, weepholes were often provided to drain any water that entered. As with stone and brick masonry, systems of flashing were developed in attempts to prevent water from entering the terra-cotta work in the first place.

CERAMIC VENEER

In the 1930s, the manufacture of terra-cotta was revolutionized by the development of machinery to produce an extruded terra-cotta panel called ceramic veneer. Ceramic veneer was prepared by extruding a deaired mixture of clay and water under high pressure through dies to form slugs of the approximate size required. The roughened backs of the slugs had dovetailed slots for keying or the installation of anchors. When the slugs were dry, surfaces to be exposed were machine-planed flat and smooth. After surfacing, a ceramic finish was applied, and the material was fired in the usual manner. Drawn from the kiln, the slugs were sawn into their required shapes using modern stone-fabricating methods, producing panels with true surfaces and accurate dimensions. Geometrical ornamentation with shallow relief in one direction was also possible with this material.

More homogeneous than terra-cotta, ceramic veneer was stronger and could be furnished in larger units. It could be used for large plane surfaces without fear that the material would warp during firing. Another advantage was the additional space possible on the interior of a building because the cladding was at least 2-1/2 inches thinner than terra-cotta panels.

Ceramic veneer was attached in two ways. Slabs could be anchored to a grid of small metal rods, which were fastened to a masonry or concrete surface. The entire space between the back of the veneer and the face of the backup masonry was then filled with lean grout. Smaller units could be directly adhered to a masonry or concrete surface. Pieces were buttered with mortar and tapped into place against the backup structure.

PROPERTIES

Terra-cotta's many positive qualities include the ease with which the plastic clay can be modelled into almost any shape and the durability, lightness, economy, ability to accept colorful glazes, and resistance to fire and weathering of the finished product. Terra-cotta can be made to imitate other materials such as stone or brick. Among the qualities that make terra-cotta difficult to use are its tendency to warp and shrink irregularly in firing and its brittleness. It is also highly susceptible to damage from internal stresses caused by the absorption of water. Glazed terra-cotta can be affected by the different reactions of the clay body and the surface glaze to expansion of the body, as well as to outside factors such as variations in temperature.

DETERIORATION AND EVALUATION OF TERRA-COTTA MASONRY

An evaluation of the condition of architectural terra-cotta will reveal the extent and severity of the deterioration, whether it involves the visual aspects of the terra-cotta surface only, the failure of joints between terra-cotta units, the structural failure of the units themselves, the failure of support systems, or the structural stability of the building façade itself.

Inspecting and Evaluating Terra-Cotta Masonry

Terra-cotta masonry should be inspected for the elements of deterioration such as joint and glaze failure, cracks and splits, missing sections, deteriorated anchors, and failure of subsurface structural elements.

In addition to visual inspection, tapping the terra-cotta blocks with a rubber- or acrylic-headed mallet can indicate hidden deterioration, particularly the separation of the surface shell from the internal webs. In general, units that have a clear, quick response to the mallet are sound, while units that have a dull response have separated. Blocks that are suspended in building elements such as lintels and cornices are particularly susceptible to interior separations because of their location and construction. Metal detectors can be used to locate anchors and give some indication of their conditions. The absence of a signal or a weak signal can indicate that the anchors have corroded or that no anchors exist in a selected area. Strain relief testing can reveal the amount of strain in a section of the terra-cotta cladding.

Hairline cracking can also indicate a major structural defect. Terra-cotta is brittle, and hairline cracks destroy the structural integrity of the hollow block, making it possible for sections to detach easily. Cracking may result from stresses caused by anchorage failure and/or slippage and buckling. Serious cracks may be isolated to one unit or may occur in patterns through several units. The cumulative weight of a section of a wall may exert pressure on a number of blocks, forcing them to move outwardly away from the wall once they have cracked.

As with other façade materials, numerous factors may be involved in the deterioration of architectural terra-cotta. Inherent faults in the material, poor detailing, improper installation, and the effects of exposure and outside influences can all be causes of failure of the terra-cotta itself and of the wall system of which it is a part.

Deterioration Related to the Properties of Terra-Cotta and Its Environment

The most basic cause of deterioration (but one that is rarely structurally significant) is the failure of the burned clay body itself. Occlusions in the clay, improper clay selection, inadequate mixing, and underfiring or overfiring are all conditions that can lead to a product unable to perform its function on the façade.

The development of glazed terra-cotta introduced its own set of problems; many terra-cotta failures occur in buildings constructed between 1895 and 1920 when glazing was common. The applied exterior coating has thermal properties different from those of the terra-cotta body, and differential stresses exist between the two. If the coefficient of thermal expansion of the glaze is less than that of the clay, a state of compression is introduced into the glaze, inhibiting crazing; thus, the most stable terra-cotta has glaze under mild compression. If, on the other hand, the surface of the body contracts less than the glaze, tension develops in the glaze, which is relieved by hairline cracking. These relationships further change when moisture is present. When the glaze is strained, spalling can be expected.[2] The relationship between the glaze and the clay body can be evaluated by an experienced petrographer.

Glaze also acts as a vapor barrier. Moisture can pass into porous terra-cotta through hairline cracks in the glaze; water can enter the material from sources behind the glaze; and water vapor can condense in the material. Moisture builds up in the terra-cotta body when it cannot evaporate through the glaze. Crystals of salts or ice can form beneath the glaze, exerting pressure that may lead to bonding failure, in which the glaze separates from the body. The resulting exposed sections of the terra-cotta body allow moisture to be absorbed, and the process of deterioration then feeds on itself. As more sections fail, more water enters, accelerating the process of decay and leading to corrosion of the anchoring system.

Exposure to the elements may also take its toll on terra-cotta construction primarily by the action of moisture through freeze/thaw cycles, acidic atmospheric conditions, and acid rain. Continuous exposure to carbon dioxide and sulphuric dioxide may dull the glaze.

Deterioration Related to Improper Design, Specifications, or Workmanship

Deterioration may also be caused by problems in the design of details, unsuitable specifications, and poor workmanship. In some cases, the architect's misunderstanding of the material may have resulted in faults designed into the whole system of terra-cotta units, the mortar or sealant filling the joints between them, the anchors or ties restraining the units, and the supporting structure. If, for example, the system failed to support the blocks properly while allowing for relief of stresses caused by thermal movement of the blocks and the façade elements around them, stresses created by these forces may lead to failure. One of the most critical requirements in the design of terra-cotta construction is to provide for movement of the terra-cotta elements, especially important in multistory structures. Where terra-cotta blocks have been too rigidly connected to the masonry backing or metal supporting structure, substantial vertical cracking may occur to relieve the stresses caused by thermal movement or expansion due to water absorption. This cracking accelerates weathering and deterioration. Once either the terra-cotta itself has cracked or the joints between the pieces have failed, water entering behind the surface may corrode ferrous metal anchors. (Fig. 5.5) By the 1920s, flexible joints and properly designed shelf angles were being recommended but were not always used, and even when they were, they sometimes did not perform adequately.[3]

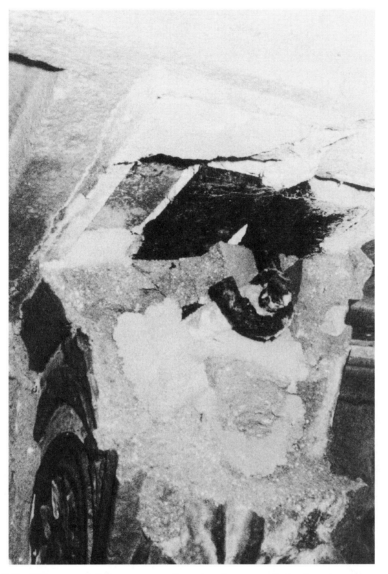

FIGURE 5.5. *This corroded ferrous metal anchor has caused the deterioration and loss of the terra-cotta unit it previously fastened to the building.* Ricardo Viera, Senior Conservator, Building Conservation Associates, Inc.

Failure may also occur because the wall was not properly designed to exclude water or to permit water that found a point of entry to escape without causing harm. When terra-cotta absorbs moisture, it, like other clay products, expands at varying rates. This expansion is not completely reversible by drying at atmospheric temperatures. If this expansion is constrained, as would be the case either where the body of glazed terra-cotta blocks has a coefficient of thermal expansion greater than that of the glaze or where large areas of terra-cotta facing lack resilient joints to allow for expansion, the terra-cotta may be compressed. The compressive stresses may cause cracking and bulging of the terra-cotta units.

Improper installation, such as out-of-level or -plumb construction, and poorly filled mortar joints may cause additional stresses. If the building's structure was not adequately designed to resist wind loading, pressure from wind-induced movement may have placed the material on the side of the building that is facing into the wind in tension, causing the joints to open so that moisture can penetrate. Or the material on the side away from the wind may have been placed in compression, introducing stresses into the cladding that may contribute to deterioration.[4]

Terra-cotta assemblies also may fail because the mortar or sealant in the joints is not able to exclude water or because the mortar transferred harmful stresses or constrained the movement of units with changes in temperature and humidity.

Deterioration Related to Improper Maintenance

The most significant problems related to maintenance are usually the result of the failure to properly repair deteriorated flashings, mortar joints, and sealant joints to keep water from penetrating behind the surface. Improper cleaning of the terra-cotta may also have caused problems. Abrasive cleaning may have removed the hard outer surface; the material should never be sandblasted. Commercially available cleaners containing hydrofluoric acid may have etched the glaze, removing surface sheen. Or severe applications of these cleaners may have removed the glaze entirely. Alkaline cleaners, though probably not harmful to the glaze, may be the source of salts creating efflorescence or subflorescence if they were absorbed into the material.

REPAIR OF TERRA-COTTA MASONRY

Minor Repair

If damage to the terra-cotta portions of the façade is not too severe—that is, if it has not progressed far enough to cause deterioration to the blocks, supports, or structure—various minor repairs, including pointing and sealing deteriorated joints, surface consolidation, cutting and sealing mortar joints to relieve stress, and composite patching, may be undertaken.

Repointing or Caulking Joints. The most basic repair is repointing or caulking deteriorated joints between terra-cotta blocks. As in all repointing work, three major criteria must be met. The repointing should reestablish the surface continuity of the wall, leaving no openings through which water can enter; the mortar should be softer, and have a lower compressive strength than the terra-cotta, so that stresses in the wall will cause the mortar joint, and not the masonry, to fail; and the mortar should be appropriate in appearance, matching the original in color and texture. Installation of sealants requires selection of the proper product for the joint conditions, thorough joint preparation, and proper workmanship during the installation. Further discussion is found in Chapter 7, Mortar, and Chapter 12, Caulks and Sealants.

Relieving Stress. Terra-cotta that cracks or bulges because metallic anchors have corroded usually requires removal. Stress cracking, however, is often a condition that extends over a greater surface area and can be repaired in place by providing expansion joints, provided that the terra-cotta blocks are adequately supported. Expansion joints can be introduced by cutting along existing solid joints and caulking with an elastic sealant. If the wall is subject to movement, any open or cracked joints should also be filled with elastic sealant. Although the sealant will help eliminate the buildup of stress by allowing the terra-cotta blocks to expand and contract, it may trap water in the units because it is vapor-impermeable. When sealants are used, special care should be taken to keep water from entering the units in the first place, and to provide weepholes at the bottom of joints so that any water that does enter can escape. If the units are glazed so that they are impermeable, the weepholes may not provide enough opportunity for the water to escape. It is important also that the supporting structure is not disturbed and that anchors are not cut when the joints are opened.

Coatings. If the surface slip layer or glaze of the terra-cotta has been lost or has deteriorated, but the clay body is sound (as is often the case), the surface can be coated to restore its integrity and protect the more porous clay body from water. Only coatings with high water vapor-permeability should be used to ensure that any water vapor entering the terra-cotta can escape through the surface. The coating should also be stable in ultraviolet light and selected to match the appearance of the terra-cotta surface in color, gloss, and light reflectance. Unglazed units can often be covered with a clear coating; glazed units require a coating tinted to match the color of the glaze. Both silicate-based coatings and methyl methacrylates have been successfully applied to terra-cotta units. (Fig. 5.6)

Preparation of the terra-cotta surface should include removing broken, blistering, and failing glaze or slip, and cleaning the surface of oil, grease, and other substances that might interfere with the coating's adherence. The coating should be applied to a dry surface following manufacturer's directions for method of application and environmental conditions required during application.

Patching. Standard composite masonry patching techniques are not easy to use for patching terra-cotta because of the difficulty in matching the texture and color of the clay surface, as well as that of any glaze present. In addition, a basic incompatibility between

FIGURE 5.6. *The glaze on this terra-cotta unit is being repaired with a dental composite material cured using a fiber-optic light source.* Kevin Daley, Conservator, Building Conservation Associates, Inc.

cement and terra-cotta can lead to cracking at the joint between the original piece and the patch, and to failure of any applied coating. Some manufacturers have recently developed proprietary modified cementitious patching mixes that can be formulated in special colors for use in filling small areas of damaged terra-cotta.

Broken terra-cotta has been successfully patched with mixes based on synthetic resins, but because epoxy and acrylic resins discolor badly upon prolonged exposure to sunlight, the patches must be protected from ultraviolet rays with a coating that matches the surface of the adjacent terra-cotta. As with all patching on existing masonry, proper surface preparation and adherence to product manufacturer's directions is essential.

Previous Repairs. If terra-cotta has been improperly repaired in the past, it may be necessary to remove incompatible material, such as cement patches. Sometimes it will be impossible to remove impervious coatings without using a procedure, such as abrasive blasting, that is damaging to the remaining terra-cotta. In such cases, all options should be evaluated to decide whether the previous treatment is causing so much damage to the terra-cotta that it must be removed, although the terra-cotta will be damaged and will have to be patched, or whether the previous treatment should be left and any possible problems handled in some other way.

Major Repair

Areas of severe deterioration require major repairs, including filling cracks in individual pieces to reestablish the integrity of the blocks, removing individual pieces and installing new anchoring systems to replace those that have failed or deteriorated, and replacing damaged or missing pieces.

Securing Cracked Terra-Cotta. Cracked pieces of terra-cotta may be secured with reinforced resins. If the surface cracks do not affect the anchoring system, they can be filled by injecting a resin with characteristics as close as possible to those of the original material. If the anchoring system is suspect, blocks may be drilled and anchored in place with metal tubes or bolts grouted in epoxy.

When the anchors have deteriorated, the terra-cotta blocks must be removed, the anchors replaced with nonferrous anchors allowing sufficient movement, and the terra-cotta reinstalled or replaced.

Replacing Missing Pieces. A number of options exist for replacing broken or missing pieces of terra-cotta. It is generally preferable to replace damaged material with new units of the same material, in this case, terra-cotta. (Fig. 5.7) If, for some reason, use of new terra-cotta units matching the original is not feasible, possible substitute materials include cast stone, glass-fiber-reinforced plastic or cement, and stone.

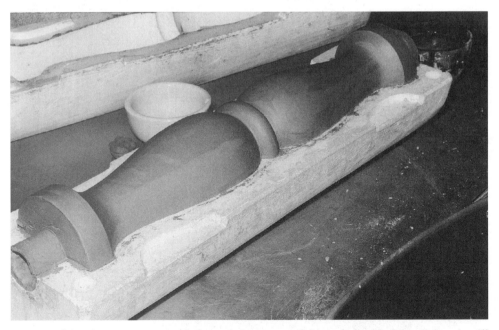

FIGURE 5.7. *A new terra-cotta baluster being removed from the mold. After firing, it will be installed to replace a deteriorated unit.* Raymond M. Pepi, President, Building Conservation Associates, Inc.

FIGURE 5.8. *New cast stone units are being used to replace the deteriorated original terra-cotta units.* Ricardo Viera, Senior Conservator, Building Conservation Associates, Inc.

New Terra-Cotta Units. Replacement with new terra-cotta units is relatively expensive. New units cannot be made from molds cast from the existing units because shrinkage during firing requires that the mold be larger than the finished piece. If the sections are deeply modelled, involving undercutting in more than one direction, they must be formed by hand in the traditional manner. New units must be carefully made to match the original in size and profile, as well as surface color and texture.

Cast Stone. When cast stone is used as a replacement material, molds can be made directly from the existing terra-cotta units because the cast material does not shrink significantly while curing. However, since cast stone is much heavier than terra-cotta, new stresses may be applied to the supporting structure and to the remaining original masonry units, particularly in areas where many units are replaced. It can also be difficult to provide cast stone matching the color and texture of the terra-cotta. Even if the surface of the original can be successfully matched, over the long term, cast stone is susceptible to weathering, which exposes the aggregate, changing the texture and light reflectance and thus the apparent color. If an acrylate finish is applied to simulate a terra-cotta surface, periodic recoating will be required. In spite of the difficulty of this procedure, it has been successfully performed on many buildings. (Fig. 5.8)

Glass-Fiber-Reinforced Cement. Units of concrete reinforced with special alkali-resistant fibers can be made thinner and lighter than regular cast stone units. They can be painted with an appropriate coating to match the original terra-cotta.

Glass-Fiber-Reinforced Plastic. Glass-fiber-reinforced resins are easily molded, lightweight, and weather-resistant. Usually, they must be coated to match the terra-cotta in appearance and to protect them from deterioration caused by ultraviolet rays. This material burns and smokes readily, but these are not major drawbacks for small repairs or for the replacement of selected individual terra-cotta blocks.

CLEANING TERRA-COTTA MASONRY

A full discussion of masonry cleaning, including evaluation of the substrate and soiling, on-site and laboratory testing, methods of cleaning, and safety precautions, is included in Chapter 3, Stone Masonry. As is the case with all building materials, terra-cotta masonry should be cleaned using the gentlest method possible so that the materials are not damaged, and overcleaning should always be avoided.

Abrasive cleaning methods should not be used on terra-cotta because they damage the surface of the material. And because the surface of glazed terra-cotta can be damaged by acidic and alkaline cleaning solutions, water washing and detergent cleaning are most appropriate. With unglazed terra-cotta, chemical cleaning solutions can be tested when detergent cleaning and water washing are not effective. On the terra-cotta of historic buildings, chemical cleaning should be used in conjunction with water washing.

Acidic cleaners containing dilute mineral and/or organic acids have been used to remove heavy soiling from unglazed terra-cotta. The cleaning process involves applying the diluted cleaner to the prewetted surface and allowing a short dwell period. Residual cleaning chemical and soiling residues are removed by pressure water rinsing. With this process, great care should be taken to avoid damage to the surfaces of the terra-cotta and to mortar, which can be attacked by acids. Sometimes, alkaline cleaners are used to clean heavy soiling on terra-cotta surfaces, but the type and strength of chemical cleaner should be selected with care and tested in small areas before major cleaning is begun.

The inappropriate or indiscriminate use of chemical cleaning can result in irreversible damage to terra-cotta. In addition, during chemical cleaning, precautions must be taken to protect workers from exposure to potential health hazards caused by chemicals and to provide proper collection and disposal of the effluent.

NOTES

1. Charles E. White, *Architectural Terra Cotta* (Scranton, 1920), 1.
2. Theodore H.M. Prudon, "Architectural Terra Cotta: Analyzing the Deterioration Problems and Restoration Approaches," *Technology and Conservation*, III, n.3 (Fall 1978), 33.
3. Prudon, 32.
4. Prudon, 35.

6

CAST STONE

Contributions by Frances Gale

CAST STONE, SOMETIMES CALLED artificial stone, architectural stone, or architectural precast concrete, is a cast, manufactured masonry material consisting of binders, aggregates, and possibly pigments, whose exterior face has a finished surface. The surface may be smooth or textured, polished or matte, and have either the natural color produced by the binders and aggregates or almost any color imparted by pigments added to the mix or by a coating applied to the cured units. It can be made to resemble stone, terra-cotta, and other building materials. Blocks of cast stone can be either reinforced or unreinforced depending on their configurations and intended uses. The material is most commonly used for copings, lintels, and sills, and as a nonbearing facing.

Joints between cast stone blocks are filled with mortar or sealant. These materials are discussed in Chapters 7 and 12, respectively.

HISTORICAL BACKGROUND

The ancient Romans are credited as the first to build with a material using a natural cement binder. They combined lime and pozzolana, a volcanic ash found in the area of Mount Vesuvius, to produce a cement that hardened under water, called hydraulic cement. This cement was mixed with sand and larger aggregates to form concrete, with which they constructed aqueducts, bridges, and buildings. After the fall of Rome, the art of building with concrete was lost until the 18th century. Until portland cement was patented in England in 1824, lime and gypsum were the only widely available binding materials.

After reinforced concrete was invented in 1868, techniques for making artificial stone developed. In the United States, early products were used for stair treads, copings, lintels, window sills, and areas where it was difficult to build with stone, or to obtain long lengths of it. From a distance, the material could be mistaken for stone; the color of the natural cement was similar to that of many light stones, and the surface texture could be varied by using different aggregates. As with terra-cotta, the material was cast in molds so that many copies could be made from one original, making it more economical to produce ornamental elements of cast stone than of stone. Unlike terra-cotta, cast stone could be produced in a mold taken directly from an original element since its minimal shrinkage did not require an enlarged model, further reducing the cost. The material was used for casting sculpture and ornament for exterior applications. (Fig. 6.1)

The development of nonfading limeproof colors after World War I made possible the production of cast stone in colors to imitate many different stones. Cast stone was increasingly used for large-scale decorative treatment because the cost of using natural stone had risen so greatly and sufficient and adequate craftspeople became harder to find. In the years just before World War II, new surface effects were achieved by incorporating stone aggregates and chips of the desired color and texture into the mixture, and then grinding and polishing the surface.

FIGURE 6.1. *Cast stone was increasingly used for ornamental façade elements beginning in the early 20th century.* James V. Banta, New York Landmarks Conservancy

PROPERTIES

As a mixture of sand, crushed rock, and other aggregates held together by a cement binder, cast stone is similar to concrete. When properly proportioned dry ingredients are combined with the right amount of water, the mixture forms a plastic mass, which can be cast or molded. Upon hydration of the cement by the water, the mixture becomes stone-like in strength, hardness, and durability.

The varying characteristics of cast stone depend on the ingredients and proportions of the mix, and on the techniques used for mixing, placing, finishing, and curing. Like other cementitious materials, cast stone possesses good compressive strength but poor tensile strength, unless it is reinforced with a tensile material such as wire, metal mesh, rods, or glass fibers. Admixtures to reduce the water content of the mixture and to improve its flow in the mold can be added.

MANUFACTURE

The first step in the manufacture of artificial stone is to make an accurate model of the shape to be cast, including provisions for the required anchors, inserts, and holes. A mold is then made from the model. After any required reinforcing is placed in the mold, the correct proportions of cement, aggregates, pigments, and water are mixed and either tamped or poured in. If the mixture is plastic enough to be poured, the mold is vibrated to eliminate any trapped air. When the units are to have a polished finish, a mixture of cement and crushed stone, usually granite that has been graded by size and color, is used to form the surface. Mixtures with other aggregates can be used to provide different surface colors and textures. The cast stone units are moist cured to develop the strength of the mixture. After curing, the surface can be tooled, etched, or polished to achieve the desired effect.

Because cast stone is a manufactured product, it can be produced in any size and shape, and the characteristics can be controlled by the choice of material. Reinforcing, anchor bolts, inserts, and slots or holes for anchoring can be carefully integrated so that units can be economically mass-produced.

INSTALLATION

The types of attachment systems for cast stone include those previously developed for stone and terra-cotta using metal rod or strap anchors, as well as new methods made possible by the nature of the material and the way it is made. Bolts with washers, for example, can be cast into the pieces so that it is only necessary to add a washer and a nut to secure a piece in place.

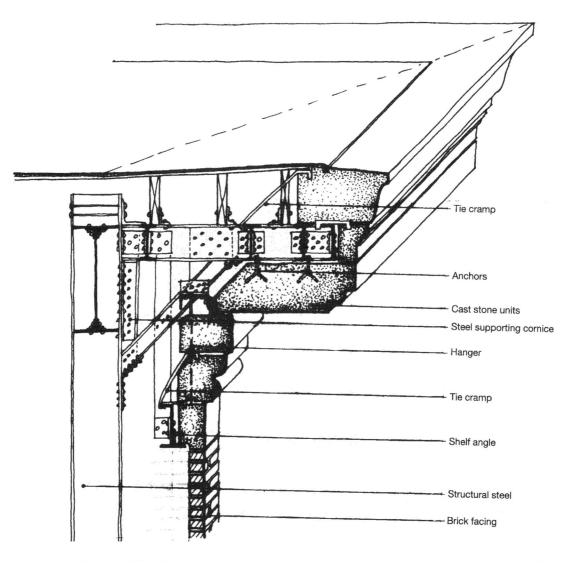

Tie cramp

Anchors

Cast stone units

Steel supporting cornice

Hanger

Tie cramp

Shelf angle

Structural steel

Brick facing

FIGURE 6.2. *Cast stone cornice elements supported by steel structural members attached to the building frame.*

Elaborate steel systems for supporting major projecting elements from a building's structural system are much like those developed for stone and terra-cotta. (Fig. 6.2) Cast stone is heavier than terra-cotta, however, and requires more counterweighting. On the other hand, because reinforced cast stone has a much higher tensile strength than either stone or terra-cotta, some large projecting elements, such as those for cornices and balustrades, can be cantilevered from the plane of the wall without projecting structural frameworks.

DETERIORATION OF CAST STONE

Evaluation of Condition

The evaluation of the condition of cast stone within a building façade will reveal the extent and severity of the deterioration, whether it involves the visual aspects of the unit's surface, structural failure of the material, or the structural stability of the building itself. The façade should be inspected for elements of deterioration such as joint failure, coating failure, cracks and splits, missing sections, deteriorated anchors, and failure of structural elements. The evaluation of mortar joints is covered in Chapter 7.

Causes of Deterioration

Like those of any manufactured material, the properties of cast stone are affected both by product design and by quality control during the manufacturing process. If the cement, aggregates, and water were incorrectly proportioned, the resulting cast stone may be weak. The same may be true if the materials were not properly mixed, if the mold was not properly vibrated to remove air bubbles, or if the unit was not properly cured. Cast stone units containing more than one color can sometimes fail because the mixes are incompatible. Incompatible reinforcing may have affected the cast stone over a period of time. Steel has a coefficient of expansion similar to that of concrete. If another metal was used for reinforcing, it may have expanded or contracted at a rate different from that of the concrete, causing stresses and possible cracking.

The cast stone elements may have failed because they were not properly installed and lacked proper provisions for structural support, water exclusion, or expansion and contraction. Commonly used ferrous anchors and supports may have oxidized and, eventually, failed. Depending on the details, the failure of the anchors may have caused the cast stone to split and the supporting structure to fail. When the material split, water may have entered and accelerated the deterioration.

The reasons for failures in excluding water from cast stone facings are similar to those encountered with other masonry materials. Joints may not have been properly designed and executed. Adequate flashings and moisture barriers may have been omitted. Poor mortar joints between cast stone units, or between cast stone units and other elements, may have allowed water to enter and corrode anchors, and, if the units became saturated, to cause rusting of ferrous reinforcing. Pointing and grouting may be poor because it was done in freezing weather.

Although cast stone can be a durable, permanent material, it is subject to atmospheric conditions and changes such as freeze/thaw cycles. When cast stone units saturated with water freeze, the forces of the expanding water can destroy them. The signs of failure are normally a crumbling, spalling, or disintegration of the unit, or a cracking of the unit around the anchoring system.

Cast stone may be subject to chemical attack as well, suffering failures similar to those of calcium-carbonate-based stones such as limestone and marble. Acids in precipitation or formed on the material by dry deposition combined with atmospheric moisture may have damaged the surface. Other acids carried in water introduced into the wall from rain, rising damp, or condensation may also have attacked the material. Soluble salts may have crystallized in the pores of the cast stone, producing expansive forces that caused the material to fail in a manner similar to that caused by water during repeated freeze/thaw cycles.

REPAIR OF CAST STONE

Minor Repair

The simplest repair of a cast stone surface is the pointing of the joints as discussed in Chapter 7, Mortar. Where there is an obvious need to relieve stress or where movements are expected, an elastomeric sealant can be used. A properly applied sealant will provide the joints with the flexibility needed to withstand expansion/contraction cycles. Sealants are discussed in Chapter 12.

Surface Repairs

Cast stone that has weathered and deteriorated can be consolidated using techniques similar to those used for stone consolidation. Standard masonry patching techniques—discussed in Chapter 3, Stone Masonry—using composite patches and dutchmen are applicable for small repairs of deteriorated cast stone as long as the color, texture, and other physical properties of the original material are matched. To ensure that the patch will survive atmospheric changes, the new material should have the same thermal coefficient and permeability as the older material. Cracked pieces may be secured with compatible reinforced resins.

Reinforcing Repairs

If repairs are required because deteriorated reinforcing has caused the surface to spall or crack, additional measures may be necessary. The deterioration of the reinforcing can be either relatively minor or major. It is minor if it has caused damage to the cast stone unit but has not significantly affected its strength; it is major if it has weakened the cast stone unit so that it is no longer able to fulfill its function. Minor deterioration of the reinforcing can be repaired by removing all deteriorated metal and protecting remaining material with a waterproof coating such as an epoxy paint. The cast stone can then be patched as previously described. Extensive deterioration of the reinforcing requires major repair.

Major Repair

Areas of severe deterioration require major repairs such as securing or replacing damaged or missing pieces or reinforcing pieces in which the reinforcing has severely deteriorated. If the reinforcing has corroded sufficiently to affect the strength of the unit, new reinforcing can be installed and composite patching applied to the surface, but it would probably be more cost-effective to replace the unit. The deteriorated original reinforcing must be protected so that it will not continue to deteriorate, to expand, and to spall off the surface of the block. In the case of deteriorated anchors, the units must be removed to allow for their replacement. If the blocks are usable, they can be reinstalled; if not, new pieces will have to be cast.

Because cast stone is a manufactured product, it should not be difficult to provide new units matching the original units if proper care is taken in selecting aggregates and pigments. Special sizes and shapes can be made, and the characteristics can be controlled by the choice of ingredients. Molds can be made directly from the existing units, as there

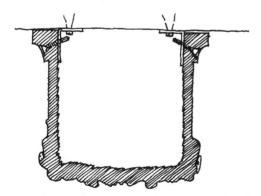

FIGURE 6.3. *Major repair of cast stone may involve replacement with newly cast pieces made from glass-fiber-reinforced cement.*

is no significant shrinkage. All reinforcing in replacement units exposed to the weather should be stainless steel or alkali-resistant glass fiber. Deteriorated cast stone units can also be replaced with units made from glass-fiber-reinforced cement or from glass-fiber-reinforced plastic. (Fig. 6.3)

Coatings

Various coatings, such as silicate paints, can be applied to cast stone units. They must be vapor-permeable, compatible with the products in the cast stone and mortar or sealant, and applied after any patches to the cast stone have fully cured and the surfaces have been properly prepared.

CLEANING CAST STONE MASONRY

A full discussion of masonry cleaning, including evaluation of the substrate and soiling, on-site and laboratory testing, methods of cleaning, and safety precautions, is included in Chapter 3, Stone Masonry. Considerations for cleaning cast stone masonry are similar to those for cleaning calcareous stones such as limestone and marble. Cast stone masonry has been cleaned with water washing, with or without soaking, or by chemical cleaning with detergent solutions. For heavy soiling, alkaline cleaners are sometimes used to soften or break down encrusted deposits enabling removal with water rinsing. An acidic solution and additional water rinsing should be used to neutralize the surface.

The gentlest possible method of cleaning should be used to avoid damage to the cast stone. The substrate and soiling should be carefully evaluated, and proposed methods should be tested on small areas of masonry before general cleaning is begun.

7

MORTAR

MORTAR, AN ESSENTIAL COMPONENT of masonry construction using stone, brick, terra-cotta, or cast stone, is an adhesive material obtained by mixing the proper proportions of an aggregate and a binder with water until the mixture is plastic and homogeneous. Sand is the most common aggregate; cement, lime, or a combination of cement and lime are the most common binders. The mortar functions as a bed for each unit in a masonry wall, allowing for the surface irregularities of the masonry units, and acts as a glue, bonding the individual masonry units together.

BINDERS

Natural Lime

The earliest masonry construction used mortar with a binder of lime. The lime was produced by burning limestone or oyster shells, the principal component of which is calcium carbonate (calcite), to yield calcium oxide, sometimes called burnt lime, and carbon dioxide. Mixing the burnt lime powder with water produces calcium hydroxide, also known as slaked or hydrated lime. Slaked lime in water is called lime putty. When the putty is exposed to the atmosphere, it reacts with carbon dioxide in the air to form calcite. Lime mortar is a mixture of lime putty and sand. Cured lime mortar, therefore, is sand in a calcite matrix. The cycle from calcium carbonate to calcium oxide to calcium hydroxide and back to calcium carbonate can be represented as follows:

$$CaCO_3 \rightarrow CaO + CO_2$$
$$CaO + H_2O \rightarrow Ca(OH)_2$$
$$Ca(OH)_2 + CO_2 \rightarrow CaCO_3$$

Historically, natural lime was usually prepared on the job site, and its preparation was sometimes hazardous. Because the slaking process is an exothermal reaction, the addition of burnt lime to water sometimes caused violent spattering of a caustic liquid. Lime putty was also messy.

Manufactured Lime

Efforts to develop a material that was easier to work with and more consistant resulted in factory-hydrated lime. The composition of this lime could be carefully controlled, and the mason could work with dry, safe ingredients. However, factory hydration requires a purer lime to start with, so only the purest lime can be used. Unfortunately, pure white lime is also the softest and weakest. The development of factory-made hydrated lime (around 1910) coincided with the spreading use of artificial cements, of which portland cement is the best known. The addition of cements to mortars made with pure white lime provided strength that had formerly been supplied by impurities in the lime.

Hydrated lime in powder form became so successful that it is now the primary type of lime commercially available in the United States. Recently, however, factory-slaked lime putty packaged in barrels has been introduced. Hydraulic lime is also available. An approximation of historic lime mortars can be made by adding some cement to hydrated lime before mixing it with other ingredients.

Portland Cement

Portland cement, patented in England in 1824, has been manufactured in the United States since 1871. It became a major ingredient in mortar after 1880. Mortar using portland cement is strong and hard and absorbs less water than does lime mortar.

MORTARS

The earliest type of mortar used in load-bearing masonry construction in the United States was a mixture of lime and sand—a mortar used predominantly until about 1880. It was soft enough to allow movement and flexibility in the masonry components to compensate for uneven settlement of foundations, movement of other structural elements, or thermal or moisture stresses.[1] If stresses induced by settlement or other causes did occur, the wall could move or bend a little without causing cracks in the joints. If overstressed joints did develop small cracks, the lime mortar would readhere and seal the cracks after a few rains through a process called autogenous healing.

Lime mortars were especially compatible with the soft brick produced from many of the early kilns. Because the mortar was softer than the brick, it would move or crack, allowing the load to be redistributed, rather than resist the forces, until both brick and mortar cracked. A general rule for all masonry is that the mortar should be softer than the stone or clay units it joins. It should also be compatible with these materials in other ways, including vapor-permeability.

Several important changes occurred in the use of mortar in the late 19th century. As bricks used in load-bearing construction became stronger, so did the mortar used to bind them as the lime was replaced by cement. As buildings became larger, more quality control was applied in the mixing of mortars at centralized plants, allowing for more accurate measurement by weight rather than by volume as is usual in the field. After 1880, a broader range of building materials and structural systems that required new properties in mortar were introduced. In taller buildings, as masonry evolved from a structural material to a cladding material, cement mortars used were stronger, more rigid, and less yielding than the lime mortars used in earlier construction.

The use of hard cement mortars is universal in new construction today. Because they transfer stresses to the masonry units, they are more appropriate for use with concrete blocks and harder and denser modern bricks, which can withstand far greater forces before breaking than could the bricks of the 18th and the greater portion of the 19th centuries. At first, cement-based mortars contained only cement and sand. Later, lime was added to improve the mortar's adhesion, make it easier to work, and produce a pore structure that allows the mortar joint to be vapor-permeable. Pure cement mortars are relatively vapor-impermeable.

Because portland cement mortars have been almost universally used in new construction during the 20th century, they have also been used to point joints in many historic masonry buildings—a use for which their high strength, inflexibility, and relative vapor-impermeability make them inappropriate. The use of such mortars between softer masonry units has caused severe deterioration of historic bricks and blocks of stone. The hardness of the mortar makes it difficult to remove from the joints without causing even further damage to the historic masonry.

Properties of mortar significant to bond development are adhesion, water retention, workability, and tensile strength. The performance of mortar depends greatly on the proportions of its ingredients. A relatively high sand content results in mortar of low strength, poor workability, and low shrinkage. A relatively high portland cement content makes high strength hard mortar of short setting time and high shrinkage. A relatively high lime content results in slower setting, good workability, less strength, and high shrinkage. Excess water will cause shrinkage of the mortar as well as high porosity.

JOINTS

Joints play different roles in bearing and nonbearing construction. In bearing walls, which are typically used in small buildings with limited wall area, a soft mortar generally provides adequate flexibility to relieve stresses that may develop throughout the system of joints if there are no major structural problems. In nonbearing applications, however, two kinds of joints are needed: those that fill the voids between units and those that are flexible enough to relieve stresses between large expanses of bonded masonry units. The concept of the latter kind of joint, called an expansion joint, was developed as problems arose with large expanses of unrelieved masonry in high-rise construction. Many early nonbearing masonry walls—including those built as late as the 1930s—may not have them. Consequently, many of these walls have failed.

The minimum required width for mortar joints is about 3/16-inch—the narrowest dimension allowing mortar to constitute a coherent material that will adhere to porous substances. The actual width of masonry joints in a particular wall depends both on the characteristics of the masonry units being joined and the aesthetic wishes of the designer. Joints need to be wide to lay rough blocks of stone in even courses. Handmade bricks are also laid with relatively wide joints—often between 3/8-inch and 1/2-inch in width. Finely dressed stone and machine-pressed bricks, which have regular dimensions, can be laid with thin "buttered" joints. The buttered joint—sometimes much less than 3/16-inch wide—was common in brickwork of the late 19th and early 20th centuries.

Different profiles are used in the finishing of brick joints both to enhance aesthetic qualities and to resist weathering. (Fig. 7.1) The simplest finish is a flush or struck joint where excess mortar is just cut off with a mason's trowel flush with the face of the wall. The most weather-resistant joint is the tooled concave joint where the mortar is well

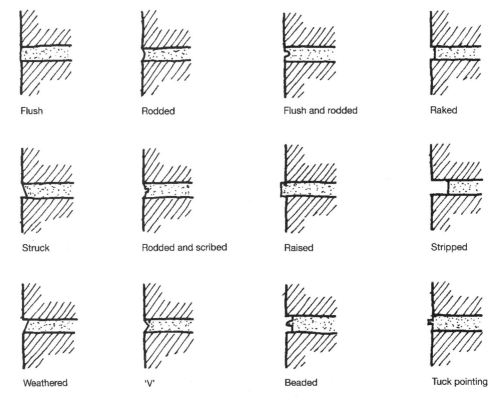

FIGURE 7.1. *Mortar joint profiles. The joint profile affects both the functional and aesthetic qualities of the masonry.*

compacted. A "raked" joint is made by raking the mortar out to a uniform depth along the joint. Although this joint treatment creates a strong shadow line for aesthetic effect, it also provides a ledge on which water can collect. Numerous other joint profiles have been used over the years.

DETERIORATION AND EVALUATION OF MORTAR AND MORTAR JOINTS

Evaluation of Condition

Minor mortar deterioration may affect only a wall's appearance, but if the deterioration is severe enough to have allowed water to enter, the water may have caused further deterioration of the mortar, the masonry units, and ties, anchors, or other elements behind the skin. If the deterioration is so great that much of the mortar is missing, it may have affected the stability of the wall directly. The deterioration may have been caused by the expansion and contraction of water during freeze/thaw cycles, by the pressure of crystallizing salts, by the gradual leaching out of the binder by water migration, by abrasion (from natural causes or from abrasive blasting), and by attack by acid rain or other chemicals that dissolve the binders. The action of these outside forces may have been accelerated if the mortar was improperly formulated or mixed or improperly applied. Another common cause of mortar joint failure is previous inappropriate repointing.

Incorrect Formulation and Application

Mortar deterioration may have occurred if the original mix was too weak because the binder-to-aggregate ratio was low or because too much water was added to the mix. In addition to being weak, a mix with too much water may have shrunk away from the masonry units. Another problem in the application may have been masonry units that were too absorptive, causing the water to be drawn out of the mortar before a good bond was formed between the mortar and the units. It is also possible that the units were too wet and not absorptive enough so that the mortar was not drawn into their pores at all, and no proper bond was made.

Joints may not have been filled properly when the units were laid. Mortar was placed only on the edges of the bed joints leaving the interior of the joints empty. (Fig. 7.2) Any water that entered may have collected in these spaces and been subject to freeze/thaw cycles. Head joints may not have been full-shoved, but buttered only on the edges so that the interior was empty; or they may have been slushed full with a mortar too wet to adhere sufficiently.

Even if the masonry was properly laid, the mortar may not have been kept damp long enough to cure properly. If it was allowed to dry out too quickly (under the noon-day sun

FIGURE 7.2. *Failure to properly apply mortar can result in deterioration of the masonry. When this wall was laid, the mortar was applied only to the edges of the bricks, leaving the middle portion of the bed joints open. Water can collect in these spaces.* Raymond M. Pepi, President, Building Conservation Associates, Inc.

FIGURE 7.3. *Cracks and losses in mortar joints can allow water to enter the masonry, and, with the effects of freeze/thaw cycles, cause masonry units to spall.* James V. Banta, New York Landmarks Conservancy

on a southern exposure, for example) it may have shrunk and cracked. On the other hand, if it rained or a direct stream of water was directed at the wall soon after the mortar was inserted, the binder may have been washed away, leaving the mortar weaker than intended.

Freeze/Thaw Cycles

Mortar is also destroyed by forces exerted on cell walls by the expansion of water during freezing. The more times that the water changes from a liquid to a solid, the more chance there is of damage to the mortar. The severity of the damage is also dependent on the amount of water entering the masonry. Thus, any cracks or openings caused by adhesion failure, shrinkage, or structural movement that allow water to enter can quickly accelerate deterioration from freeze/thaw action. (Fig. 7.3) Damage caused by water in the wall may also be the result of condensing water vapor that entered the wall from the interior of the building.

Leaching

In many masonry walls constructed with lime mortar and exposed to the weather, the lime may slowly wash from the mortar over the years. In such walls, it is not uncommon to be able to start at the top of the wall and remove the bricks one at a time with bare hands. As long as there was no movement and water did not rush down the façade to erode the mortar, walls may have existed in this condition for many years. If the mortar has been washed from the face of the joint, however, water may enter, causing deterioration in the future.

Abrasion

Abrasion of the mortar by wind-driven particles and by dust and dirt carried in water flowing over it also may wear away mortar sufficiently to affect the integrity of the joints. More serious deterioration of the joints may have been caused by abrasive blasting using sand or other abrasive particles under air pressure or using water containing sand (called hydrosilica cleaning), popular methods of cleaning masonry buildings in the past. These methods are guaranteed to damage the mortar joints, as well as the masonry units. Often, the joints had to be repointed after the building was abrasively cleaned.

Acid Rain

Lime and cement are soluble in acids, such as those formed when gases in air are dissolved in rainwater. Thus, the binders may have been dissolved out of the mortar. Acid rain is not a new problem. Even in the 19th century, rain in the cities was acidic because of the large quantities of fossil fuels burned to heat the buildings.

Waterproof Coatings

Waterproof coatings such as silicone may have led to deterioration of mortar in the joints in the same way that the coatings may have led to deterioration of the masonry units themselves. The coating may have trapped moisture behind it, causing damage from freeze/thaw cycles and trapped salts.

Previous Repointing

Because mortar deteriorates—and it is always preferable to have the mortar rather than the masonry units deteriorate—-old masonry walls may have been repointed in the past. If the mortar joints are deteriorated, they may have been improperly repointed. The original mortar may not have been removed deeply enough to allow the new mortar to form a coherent mass and bond properly to the masonry units. Or the joints may not have been properly cleaned after the mortar was removed. Mortar dust remaining in the joint would have prevented a good bond between the new mortar and the masonry units. Of course, almost any of the mistakes that could have been made with the formulation and application of the original mortar, such as using mortar that was too wet or not curing it properly, could have been made with the mixing and application of the repointing mortar. One of the most common problems found where walls have been repointed is the use of improperly hard portland cement mortar in joints between soft masonry units.

REPOINTING

The most common, and usually the simplest, repair required by masonry walls is repointing. If it is done well, repointing will both protect the building and enhance its historical character. (Fig. 7.4) The pointed masonry wall should meet three criteria. First, the continuity of the wall should be reestablished, and all voids or cracks that might allow water to enter eliminated. Second, the new mortar should be chosen and applied so that it will fail before the masonry units fail. The freezing and thawing action of any water that is able to enter the wall will cause failure in either the mortar or the masonry units depending on the relative properties and detailing of these elements. Again, the mortar rather than the masonry should fail. Third, the appearance of the wall after it has been pointed should resemble as closely as possible that of the wall as it was originally built.

FIGURE 7.4. *Repointing is a relatively simple procedure that, if properly done, will protect a façade and enhance its historic character.* Raymond M. Pepi, President, Building Conservation Associates, Inc.

As a general rule, new mortar joints should match the old in composition, color, texture, profile, strength, and hardness. It is important, however, to be sure that the old mortar was appropriate in the first place. If it was too hard, the mortar for repointing should be softer than the material that is being pointed. If the masonry units have deteriorated so that they have become softer—but not so soft that they need to be replaced—they should be repointed with softer mortar so that freeze/thaw cycles will not cause the stone to disintegrate. Many cases of stone decay have been directly traced to a situation in which a porous stone was pointed with an impervious mortar. In such cases, both the absorption and evaporation of water are confined to the stone, whereas the process should ideally be evenly distributed over the stone and pointing.[2]

Although repointing is an important step in preserving masonry buildings, it can permanently damage buildings that have stood in relatively good condition for hundreds of years. Damage caused to masonry units by carelessness during removal of remaining existing mortar, improper repointing, or repointing with an inappropriate mortar can irreparably harm both the physical structure of the building and its appearance. Inappropriate repointing is often difficult and expensive to correct; sometimes it is impossible.

Preparation

Before joints are repointed, all loose and deteriorated mortar should be removed. Even sound mortar should be removed to a depth of at least 3/4-inch so that the new mortar will be deep enough to be cohesive and to bond to the masonry units. The old mortar must be removed without damaging the existing masonry units. It is easy to chip the edges of stone blocks, bricks, or other masonry elements; it is almost impossible to properly repair them. Therefore, removal of mortar requires great care. Careful removal usually means raking the mortar from the joints with small hand tools. Chisels should fit cleanly within the width of the joint; they should never touch the edges of the masonry units. It may be possible to remove very soft mortar with the chisel only. When it is necessary to use a hammer, the chisel should be carefully aimed before each blow to ensure that no force will be applied to the masonry units.

Special pneumatic tools have been developed for use in removing mortar from joints in historic masonry. When used by skilled craftspeople, mortar can be removed even from thin joints between relatively soft stone blocks without damage to the stones.

When hard portland cement mortar must be removed or the joints are fine "buttered" joints common early in the 20th century, it may be necessary to use a small power saw with a thin diamond blade to remove the mortar. Although a skilled craftsperson can use a small saw without damaging the masonry, power tools should not be used unless they are necessary; it is easy to slip and permanently damage some of the masonry units. Care must be taken not to enlarge the joints and not to damage the units at the top and bottom of the head joints. The latter requirement usually means that the mortar remaining at the top and bottom of the head joints after the saw has been used will have to be removed with a small chisel.

After the mortar has been removed to a uniform depth or to sound mortar (whichever is greater), the joints should be thoroughly cleaned out with clean compressed air and flushed with clean water. Porous masonry units and existing mortar should be well wetted before the new mortar is inserted. If the masonry is too dry, it will rapidly absorb water from the fresh mortar, thereby reducing the bond strength. The units, however, should not be visably wet with freestanding water; excess water will weaken the mortar, hinder the absorption and thus the introduction of mortar into the pores of the masonry, and weaken the bond strength.

Mortar

When choosing the type of mortar to be used in repointing, full consideration must be given to matching the old mortar in color, texture, strength, density, and porosity, provided the original mortar was appropriate. It is important to make sure that the observed mortar was indeed the original, and not a previous repointing mortar.

When the original mortar has been identified, it can be analyzed using a simple laboratory test. Samples of the mortar are crushed and covered with an acid that dissolves all of the acid-soluble components. The remaining particles or aggregates of the mortar can then be studied. This analysis helps in identifying ingredients that will produce the desired color and texture. Aggregate sizes can be accurately measured by sieving the remains to determine the distribution of different-sized particles. The particle distribution and color of the aggregate can be matched against samples of available material. Because color and texture of repointing mortar should be determined primarily by the aggregate, care should be taken to obtain an aggregate of the proper color and size.

If it is not possible to find all of the original ingredients, it may be necessary to add pigment to produce the original color. But pigments should be used sparingly, because acid rain will dissolve the binder on the surface of the joint, removing the pigment with it. Thus, after exposure, the aggregate will be more prominent than it was when the joint was first tooled. Care must be taken so that the joints will not appreciably change color under this action. If a small amount of pigment is required to achieve the proper color, only inorganic pigments that are insoluble in water and free from acids and soluble salts should be used. They must also be nonreactive with calcium hydroxide, and have demonstrated, through exposure, that they do not fade.

Whatever the original mortar, it is important that the repointing mortar has the same density and water absorbency as the stones or bricks in the wall, and a lower compressive strength than the masonry. Soft bricks and stones should be repointed with softer mortar; hard cement mortars will cause soft brick to disintegrate. Because hard cement mortars are nonresilient and comparatively nonabsorbent, they will not respond to atmospheric conditions to the same extent as the stone or brickwork they contact. Saturation and evaporation will be confined to the stone or brick, causing great stress on the individual units. As a rule, the higher the ratio of density between bricks and mortar, the greater the degree and rapidity of brick disintegration.[3]

For the repointing of old soft-brick buildings, a lime-sand mortar mixed with portland cement in a ratio of one part cement to two or three parts lime is recommended. For harder brick walls, mortar mixes with higher cement-to-lime ratios may be used. Any mortar should have a binder to aggregate ratio of approximately 1:3. Because they often contain proprietary ingredients not found in historic mortars, pre-mixed products such as masonry cements and masonry mortars are not appropriate for use in much historic masonry.

Installation

The prepared joints should be thoroughly filled with the appropriate mortar. The mortar should be consolidated by pressing it in with the proper tools, including a long, thin trowel that is narrower than the joints. There should be no voids, and the mortar must adhere firmly to each side of the joint. Superficial pointing has no durability.

Masonry containing weathered bricks or blocks of stone with worn edges or rounded profiles must be repointed so that the face of the new mortar is recessed slightly behind the faces of the masonry units. This approach will keep the joints from becoming too wide and will avoid the spreading of mortar over the edges of the stone blocks or bricks. Edges that overlap the masonry break off easily, carrying particles of brick with them and leaving cavities through which moisture may enter. They also provide a ledge, which will catch water and allow it to enter the joint. Thus, it is important to keep the mortar off the surfaces of even hard, sharp-edged brick.

Repointed mortar joints should be tooled to match the appearance of the original joints. Brushing the surface of the new mortar gently with a stiff brush before it has set completely produces a stippled effect, which gives new mortar surfaces an appearance matching older surfaces.

Curing

Because portland cement mortar continues to gain strength over time as long as it is wet, new mortar should be kept damp for at least several days after it has been installed. Mortar that is moist will also shrink less. It is especially important to keep the new mortar damp and shaded during hot weather. It is equally important to avoid directing a stream of water at the mortar for at least 24 hours after it has been placed. Such a stream might wash the binder from the surface before it has set.

Surface Grouting or "Bagging"

A specialized form of repointing is surface grouting, which is a useful way to repair small cracks in brick walls or to fill very narrow "butter joints" in pressed brick walls. A mortar slurry or paste is rubbed into the face of mortar joints to seal cracks between bricks and mortar, thus reducing water infiltration. The excess grout is removed by wiping with a damp sponge, rags, or bags. The use of burlap bags to remove the excess grout has given this technique the name "bagging." The slurry must suitably match the composition of the original mortar. After the mortar has been allowed to cure for a few days, the entire façade is washed down with water or with a solution developed for the cleaning of new masonry to remove the surface film left by the wiping process. Surface grouting has limited value and is no substitute for proper repointing of deteriorated joints.

Joint Covers

After joints in exposed horizontal surfaces, such as copings, have been repointed, they can be further protected by the installation of metal joint covers embedded in elastomeric sealant. These covers are very effective in keeping water out of the joint. Because the sealant is not vapor-permeable, soft stones may tend to deteriorate near the joints when this method is used. Usually, however, the stone or other masonry unit used in exposed horizontal locations is relatively hard and dense in order to protect the wall beneath from water infiltration. Hard, dense units are not seriously affected by the installation of sealants.

NOTES

1. Harley J. McKee, *Introduction to Early American Masonry*, (Washington, DC, 1978), 61.
2. McKee, 72.
3. McKee, 72.

8

CONCRETE

Diane S. Kaese

HISTORICAL OVERVIEW

CONCRETE HAS BEEN USED as a construction material since ancient times. The earliest known implementation of the material was by the Romans who combined lime putty with fine volcanic ashes. These ingredients, which harden under water, are accepted as the first hydraulic cements. The Romans became quite sophisticated in the use of the material, employing it to form buildings, bridges, and portions of the aqueduct system. The material continued to be used in Spain and Africa during the Middle Ages and was brought to the New World in the early 16th century. In coastal areas from Florida to South Carolina, a combination of lime, sand, and aggregate of shells, gravel, or stone was mixed together with water and placed layer by layer into wooden forms. Each layer was tamped and allowed to dry, forming a creamy white monolithic masonry material called tapia or tabby.

Concrete was used in England as early as 1756, but the burnt lime, sand, and water combination deteriorated quickly in wet conditions and under water. In 1824, natural cements of the same kind used by the Romans were rediscovered in England. Portland cement is named for the gray English limestone found on the Isle of Portland. Natural hydraulic cement was discovered and used in the United States during the construction of the Erie Canal, which opened in 1825.

Despite its versatility and early use, concrete was not quickly accepted as a building material—perhaps because it was utilized and perceived as an engineering, rather than architectural, material, and because the available building technology was limited. The 19th-century social philosopher and architect Orson Fowler promoted the use of "gravel wall" construction for residential purposes in his publication, *A Home for All* (1853). While the use of unreinforced concrete by the military for outposts was common during the 1860s and 1870s, other construction implementations of the material were still essen-

FIGURE 8.1. *Fonthill Museum (constructed 1908–1912), located in Doylestown, Pennsylvania is a good example of the versatility of concrete.* James V. Banta, New York Landmarks Conservancy

tially novelties. By the 1880s, however, the invention of the horizontal rotary kiln by Ernest L. Ransome permitted the production of cheaper and better-quality cements. This invention, along with cold-twisted reinforcing bars patented by Ransome in 1884, led to more widespread use of reinforced concrete. By 1909, the journal *Architect and Engineer* could note that "about everything except wearing apparel and table utensils is now made of reinforced concrete."

Indeed, the properties and nature of concrete permit variety. Concrete is a combination of aggregates, water, and a binder such as cement or lime. When mixed together, these ingredients undergo a chemical reaction, and harden. The endless variety of aggregates and the different types of binders available ensure an almost limitless number of concrete formulations.

In the early 20th century, designers often used concrete for utilitarian buildings in the "factory style"—exposing the concrete structure and using expanses of glass for infill. Concrete became increasingly cost-competitive and provided a durable structure that required low maintenance. The material also provided an opportunity to inexpensively create ornamental designs on exterior surfaces. By the 1920s, reinforced concrete structures began to display the versatility of the material. (Fig. 8.1)

From the 1920s to the present, there has been great progress in understanding the technical nature of concrete. This progress has produced major advancements in quality control, higher strengths, and an understanding of the causes of concrete deterioration.

Unlike many building materials, concrete is commonly perceived as a modern, non-historic material. The timeless engineering design quality of many early concrete structures can be deceiving. Care must be taken when evaluating concrete structures to date the buildings accurately and to understand the unique mix of materials in each structure.

DETERIORATION AND EVALUATION OF CONCRETE

Environmental effects, inferior materials, poor workmanship, inherent structural design defects, and inadequate or inappropriate maintenance are the primary causes of concrete deterioration.

Environmental Effects

The belief that concrete is waterproof is inaccurate. Concrete readily absorbs moisture, and most problems with the material's durability are affected by its ability to withstand the effects of water. Exposure to rain, snow, and wind can cause weathering and erosion of the concrete surface. The freezing of water within cracks and within the body of the concrete can cause severe cracking and spalling. Atmospheric carbon dioxide and water reacting with the alkaline components found in the cement paste can cause loss of alkalinity, and the resulting formation of neutral salts leads to the deterioration of the concrete.

The presence of biological growth in concrete will hinder evaporation of moisture. Chemical by-products of the biological growth can also disintegrate the cement binder, and stresses formed by biological growth within a crack can cause the concrete to fracture. Water can also act as a carrier of chemicals into the concrete, dissolving the cement binder and eventually depositing the chemicals as the water evaporates. Pressure from crystals formed by these chemicals can rupture the pores in which they were deposited. Most early concrete, and concrete that is hand-mixed, is not air-entrained. Air-entraining helps to limit the permeability of the concrete by encapsulating air voids, and is an important deterrent to freeze/thaw deterioration.

Inferior Materials and Poor Workmanship

Much of what would be described today as poor workmanship or use of inferior materials is actually the result of the early lack of knowledge and misunderstandings regarding the chemical processes that occur as concrete is formed. Limited technical knowledge caused many poor construction practices. One that continues to this day is the addition of calcium chloride or similar additives to a mix. While the misconception that this fireproofs the concrete has been dispelled, the practice still flourishes in cold-weather construction where the salt is added to lower the freezing point of the mix.

Long-term actions of concrete, such as thermal expansion and contraction and creep, also were not initially understood. Expansion joints to accommodate building movement are common today but often are absent in historic concrete installations.

Coal cinder and crushed brick aggregates produce a porous, weak concrete. Both of these materials absorb water and change dimension often, causing enough internal forces to internally fracture the concrete. Aggregates can also react with the alkali in the concrete to form a white, gel-like surface staining. Historically, the importance of graded aggregates was not well known, and many early concretes were formed with similar-sized aggregate. This practice produced a poorly consolidated, hence weaker, concrete that was difficult to place around elements such as reinforcing bars. The importance of consolidation was also unknown, and many early concretes have large or intermittent voids. This condition (aggregate without cement paste) is called honeycombing and is prevented by vibrating the concrete as it is being placed.

Introducing impure water, calculating incorrect water/cement ratios, and other mistakes in mixing procedures on-site, often lead to problems that limit the strength and durability of the material.

Early limitations of mixing, placing, and formwork technology resulted in the common practice of placing concrete in relatively thin layers, causing cold joints to form where the new layer was placed atop the previous layer that had hardened. At the cold joints the new concrete never fully bonds to the hardened layer, so water often infiltrates the structure at these locations. In extreme cases, joints can be opened by freeze/thaw action or biological growth. While many of these construction limitations have been eliminated or minimized, cold joints are still a common problem in today's concrete construction.

Two other problems found in both historic and contemporary installations are insufficient bar cover and improper curing. Insufficient steel reinforcing bar cover allows water penetrating the concrete to reach the reinforcing bars, causing them to deteriorate and damage the concrete. Inadequate curing often leads to lower than anticipated strengths and the formation of shrinkage cracks.

Structural Design Defects

Initial design errors can lead to deterioration of concrete. Design errors can encompass both the strength of the concrete and the size and placement of reinforcing bars. Deflection of concrete is seen, especially in early structures that were built as the nature and limits of concrete as a building material were being discovered.

Too few or improperly located expansion joints can also lead to deterioration. Like structural requirements, expansion joint requirements have evolved. When used, expansion joints accommodate stresses caused by thermal movement and creep. When there are no expansion joints, movement due to these stresses can cause cracks and other forms of deterioration.

Inadequate or Improper Maintenance

As with most construction materials, water is the primary source of deterioration. Maintenance of concrete means dealing with all forms of water and the effects of water combined with other elements. The maintenance goal for concrete is to keep as much water out of the concrete as possible.

One of the main sources of water infiltration into concrete is through cracks. Deferred crack repair can cause concrete to be continuously wet. While this condition always affects the life span of the reinforcing steel, it can be more problematic in climates where freeze/thaw cycles exist. When the saturated concrete freezes, ice crystals form. The expanding crystals rupture internal pores. The application of waterproofing coatings often serves to aggravate moisture-related problems by trapping water and water vapor in the concrete.

Continued exposure to chemicals, such as those used for deicing, can also accelerate the deterioration of concrete. Chlorides carried into the concrete by water will cause deterioration of the concrete as well as the reinforcing steel.

INSPECTING FOR CONCRETE DETERIORATION

A thorough program that includes document review, visual inspection, testing, and analysis should be conducted to identify the extent and causes of concrete deterioration. The following types of deterioration are commonly found as part of a visual inspection and should be addressed in a repair plan.

Cracking

Cracking is by far the most commonly observed form of concrete deterioration. Cracks can differ in location, pattern, width, and length. Most concrete will experience cracking in its lifetime. The cause of the cracking should be identified to help determine the appropriate repair.

Surface Erosion

Excessive exposure of aggregate and minimal visible paste is an indication that the concrete has eroded. This erosion can be localized or prevalent over the entire concrete surface. Surface erosion should not, however, be confused with exposed aggregate surface finishes, which expose the aggregate for design purposes. Common causes of surface erosion are wind, salt, or water spray and inadequate drainage. Again, it is important to know the cause of the erosion because the success of the repair depends upon removing or minimizing the initial cause.

Spalling

Spalling, or the loss of concrete surface material, occurs as the result of a buildup of stresses below the surface of the concrete. The stresses become significant enough to fracture the concrete, causing pieces of concrete to disengage from the body. Rusting steel reinforcing bars and the effects of water vapor or penetrating water (freeze/thaw damage and growth of salt crystals) are two main causes of spalling. (Fig. 8.2) Poor consolidation or overfinishing of concrete will also cause a type of spalling, called scaling. Scaling occurs when the cement paste rises to the surface and forms a thin weak layer, which will deteriorate and debond from the underlying concrete.

Deflection

Deflection indicates that there is a structural problem with the concrete. There may be numerous causes for the deflection, but, as a structural problem, it is best left for design professionals to analyze and repair.

FIGURE 8.2. *Spalling that occurs on concrete façades is often caused by the corrosion of ferrous reinforcing elements within.* Diane S. Kaese, Senior Architect, Wiss, Janney, Elstner Associates, Inc.

Staining

Staining can be the result of reactions within the concrete or the result of outside factors. Rust can be caused by the deterioration of steel within the concrete or from corrosion products washing over the concrete. A white gel that hardens on the surface is the result of alkali-silica reaction. Efflorescence is typically the presence of lime (calcium hydroxide) that has leached from the concrete.

Some concrete deterioration is not visible but is easily detectible by employing simple field-testing techniques such as dragging a chain on horizontal surfaces or tapping with a metal rod or hammer. Areas of delaminated concrete will become apparent by a change in the sound produced by these instruments. Depending on the suspected problem, there are also more sophisticated methods to determine delamination, voids or internal cracking, the location and size of reinforcing bars, the strength of the concrete, and water-permeability.

Laboratory testing plays an important role in evaluating concrete. If it will be necessary to design repair mixes for the concrete, it is advisable to have concrete samples analyzed to determine its composition and characteristics. A well-equipped laboratory should be able to determine the strength, level of carbonation, porosity, presence of chlorides or other reactive materials, alkalinity, and the composition of the concrete.

MAINTENANCE AND REPAIR OF CONCRETE

The repair of concrete should take place only after causes of the deterioration have been determined. The repair plan should begin by eliminating sources of deterioration. Those sources that cannot be eliminated should be minimized or otherwise addressed as part of the repair plan. Concrete repair is usually time-consuming and costly due to the high likelihood that numerous problems need to be addressed. Short-term solutions that do not address the causes of the deterioration should be avoided, as many temporary repairs can cause additional damage to the structure and possibly mask structural problems or other safety hazards. Regardless of the age of the concrete, it is preferable to maintain as much of the original fabric as possible. However, the key issue to be addressed is whether the existing material can be repaired and conserved or must be replaced. Outlined next are basic treatments for the maintenance and the repair of typical concrete problems.

Patching

Proper preparation of existing concrete surfaces to be patched is vital to ensure long-lived patches. All loose and unsound material should be removed, leaving a rough surface with undercut edges to which the patch can adhere. All reinforcing bars in the patch area should be cleaned and immediately coated with a high-quality rust-inhibiting primer. Depending on the condition and location of the reinforcing bars, cleaning may be adequate; however, it may be necessary to replace the reinforcing bars, or, if replacement is not necessary for structural strength, to remove them.

The patch area should be cleaned of all dust and moistened with running water, wet rags, or wet sponges. A slurry coat of cement paste should be scrubbed into the surface to increase the bond of the patch. Depending on the size of the patch and the composition of the patching material, it can be applied in lifts or layers to ensure adequate compacting. Larger patches may need to be formed and vibrated to achieve consolidation.

To ensure visual continuity, the surface texture and color of the patch should match the surrounding concrete. A successful patch should be difficult to detect visually. (Fig. 8.3) Achieving the right combination of color and technique to provide a good match may require numerous test patches. It is also important to match the composition of the patch to that of the surrounding concrete. A careful match will help assure that the patch will act in a similar manner with regard to durability, strength, and thermal expansion as the surrounding concrete.

FIGURE 8.3. *Concrete is often repaired by patching, but should be better matched than this easily visible patch.* James V. Banta, New York Landmarks Conservancy.

Cracking

Consultation with a professional to determine the cause of the cracking and to assist in developing an appropriate treatment for cracking will help to minimize the impact of cracking on the concrete. Dormant (nonmoving), hairline cracks may not need repair. If the cracks are active (moving), the repair could be complicated and possibly include routing out (widening) the crack, filling it with epoxy, and applying sealants. It may also be necessary for new expansion joints to be installed to control movement. The installation of a breathable sealer (a sealer that allows water in the concrete to evaporate) may be appropriate over the entire concrete surface to inhibit water infiltration.

Surface Erosion

The repair of surface erosion should take into account the cause of the erosion. Patterns caused by winds are not easily abated, but many sources of water erosion are correctable. The face of the eroded concrete should be removed to provide a sound, uncontaminated surface for compatible patching material.

Staining

The removal of surface stains by abrasive techniques such as water or aggregate blasting is not advisable because a thin layer of the concrete surface is removed with the staining. The preferred method is to determine the type of stain and use appropriate cleaning products to remove the contaminants (this may involve the use of poultices in cases of some deeply set stains such as oils). Once the contaminants have been removed, the surface should be rinsed with clear water. For general staining, concrete can be washed with a mild acidic detergent. The cleaning solution should be scrubbed into the surface and rinsed with clear water at a moderate pressure.

Sealers

Many products marketed to professionals and homeowners claim to "waterproof" or "seal" concrete. With the exception of silane-based products, the use of waterproofing and sealing products is generally not recommended. These products trap moisture in the concrete, aggravating and accelerating most forms of concrete deterioration.

Ice Removal

The routine use of chlorides or deicing salts to melt ice on concrete is discouraged. Chlorides carried into the concrete by water will cause deterioration of the concrete as well as the reinforcing steel. This phenomenon is also observed on areas such as bridge abutments and retaining walls that are routinely splashed with water containing deicing salts. Splash guards or other temporary shielding measures can remedy the problem. All areas exposed to chlorides or deicing chemicals should be washed in the spring to minimize the effect of deicing salts.

Structural Repairs

All repairs that involve structural components of buildings, regardless of the size of the problem, should be undertaken with the assistance of a professional experienced in concrete analysis and repair.

9

Cast Iron

John G. Waite

HISTORICAL BACKGROUND

CAST IRON WAS TOO COSTLY to make in large quantities until the mid-18th century, when new furnace technology in England made it more economical for use in construction. The first architectural use of cast iron was in the form of slender, nonflammable pillars in English cotton mills in the 1790s. Similar thin columns were first used in the United States in the 1820s to support balconies in theaters and churches.

By the mid 1820s, one-story iron storefronts were being advertised in New York City. Daniel Badger, the Boston foundryman, who later moved to New York, stated that in 1842 he fabricated and installed the first rolling iron shutter for iron storefronts, which provided protection against theft and external fire. In the following years and into the 1920s, the practical cast-iron storefront would become a favorite in cities and towns from coast to coast. Not only did the storefront help support the loads of the upper floors, it also provided large show windows for the display of wares, and allowed natural light to flood the interior of the shops. More important, cast-iron storefronts were inexpensive to assemble, requiring little on-site labor.

In 1849, James Bogardus, a self-taught architect/engineer and early advocate for the use of cast iron in buildings, created something uniquely American when he erected the first structure with self-supporting, multistory exterior walls of iron. Known as the Edgar Laing Stores, this corner row of small four-story warehouses that looked like a single building was constructed in lower Manhattan in only two months. Its rear, side, and interior bearing walls were of brick; the floor framing constructed of timber joists and girders. One of the cast-iron walls was load-bearing, supporting the wood floor framing. The innovation was its two street façades of self-supporting cast iron, consisting of multiples of only a few pieces—engaged Doric columns, panels, sills, and plates—along with some applied ornamentation. (Fig. 9.1) Each component of the façades had been cast individ-

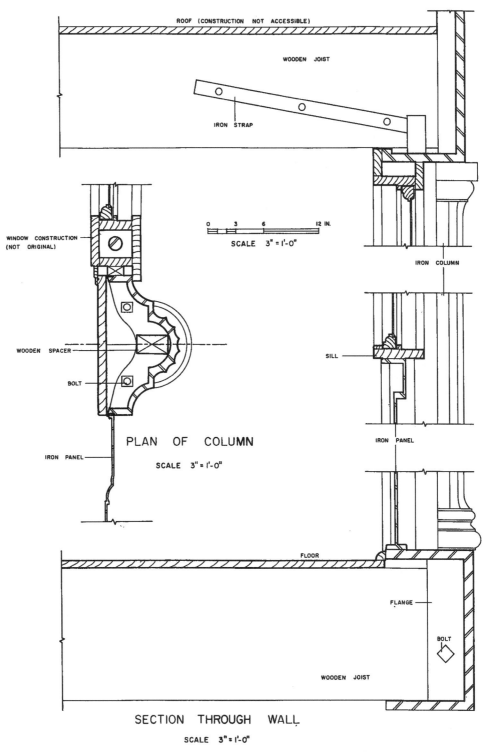

ROOF (CONSTRUCTION NOT ACCESSIBLE)

WOODEN JOIST

IRON STRAP

WINDOW CONSTRUCTION
(NOT ORIGINAL)

SCALE 3" = 1'-0"

IRON COLUMN

WOODEN SPACER

SILL

BOLT

PLAN OF COLUMN

SCALE 3" = 1'-0"

IRON PANEL

IRON PANEL

FLOOR

FLANGE

BOLT

WOODEN JOIST

SECTION THROUGH WALL

SCALE 3" = 1'-0"

FIGURE 9.1. *The Edward Laing Stores, erected by James Bogardus, was the first self-supporting multistory structure with iron exterior walls. The iron façade components cast in a foundry were assembled on site during construction.* John G. Waite, John G. Waite Associates, Architects, PLLC

ually in a sand mold, machined smooth, tested for fit, and taken on horse-drawn drays to the building site. There they were hoisted into place, then bolted together and fastened to the conventional structure of timber and bricks with iron spikes and straps. In masonry façades, cast-iron building components, such as sills and lintels, could be installed by setting them in place, much as similar stone elements might be inserted.

An iron-fronted building erected the next year was a quantum leap beyond the Laing Stores in size and complexity. Begun in April 1850 by Bogardus, the five-story Sun newspaper building in Baltimore was both cast-iron fronted and cast-iron framed.

In the second half of the 19th century, cast iron was the metal of choice for building. The use of iron in commercial and public buildings spread rapidly, and iron-fronted buildings were erected in cities across the country. (Fig. 9.2) Not only was it a fire-resistant material in a period of major urban fires, but large façades also could be produced with cast iron at less cost than comparable stone fronts. Iron buildings could also be erected with speed and efficiency. It was only at the end of the 19th century that rolled steel, which was structurally more versatile and cost-competitive, became widely available. At that time, it began to surpass cast iron for structural purposes. Nonetheless, cast iron continued to be used in substantial quantities, particularly for ornamental but also for structural purposes, well into the 20th century.

PROPERTIES

Iron is a gray-white metal, which in its pure form is relatively soft, tough, malleable, ductile, magnetic, and high in tensile strength. It oxidizes rapidly when exposed to a damp atmosphere and is readily attacked by most acids. Cast iron is an alloy with a high carbon content (at least 1.7 percent and usually 3.0 to 3.7 percent) that makes it more resistant to corrosion than either wrought iron or steel. In addition to carbon, cast iron contains varying amounts of silicon, sulfur, manganese, and phosphorus.

While molten, cast iron is easily poured into molds, making it possible to create nearly unlimited decorative and structural forms. Unlike wrought iron and steel, cast iron is too hard and brittle to be shaped by hammering, rolling, or pressing. However, because it is more rigid and more resistant to buckling than other forms of iron, it can withstand great compressive loads. Cast iron is relatively weak in tension, however, and fails under tensile loading with little prior warning.

The characteristics of various types of cast iron are determined by their composition and the techniques used in melting, casting, and heat treatment. Metallurgical constituents of cast iron that affect its brittleness, toughness, and strength include ferrite, cementite, pearlite, and graphite carbon.

Cast iron develops a kind of protective scale on its surface, which makes it more resistant to corrosion than ordinary steel. However, cast iron should be kept painted to prevent rusting.

FIGURE 9.2. *The Cary Building, 105-107 Chambers Street, built in 1856 to the design of architects Gamaliel King and John Kellum, is one of the oldest and most significant cast-iron fronted buildings in New York City. Cast by D.D. Badger's Arcitectural Iron Works, this front served as a model for dozens more built after its construction.* John G. Waite

DETERIORATION AND EVALUATION OF CAST IRON

Common problems encountered today with cast-iron construction include badly rusted or missing elements, impact damage, structural failures, broken joints, damage to connections, and loss of anchorage in masonry.

Oxidation

Also called rusting, oxidation occurs rapidly when cast iron is exposed to moisture and air. The minimum relative humidity necessary to promote rusting is 65 percent, but this figure can be lower in the presence of corrosive agents, such as sea water, salt air, acids, acid precipitation, soils, and some sulfur compounds present in the atmosphere, which act as catalysts in the oxidation process. Rusting is accelerated in situations where architectural details provide pockets or crevices to trap and hold liquid corrosive agents. Furthermore, once a rust film forms, its porous surface acts as a reservoir for liquids, which in turn cause further corrosion. If this process is not arrested, it will continue until the iron is entirely consumed by corrosion, leaving nothing but rust. (Fig. 9.3)

FIGURE 9.3. *Oxidation occurs when cast iron is exposed to air and moisture. This form of corrosion often leads to cracking, as seen in this photo.* Kim Lovejoy, New York Landmarks Conservancy

Galvanic Corrosion

Galvanic corrosion is an electrochemical action that results when two dissimilar metals react together in the presence of an electrolyte, such as water containing salts or hydrogen ions. The severity of the galvanic corrosion is based on the difference in potential between the two metals, their relative surface areas, and time. If the more noble metal (higher position in electrochemical series) is much larger in area than the base, or less noble metal, the deterioration of the base metal will be more rapid and severe. If the more noble metal is much smaller in area than the base metal, the deterioration of the base metal will be less significant. Cast iron will be attacked and corroded when it is adjacent to more noble metals such as lead or copper.

Graphitization

A less common problem, graphitization of cast iron occurs in the presence of acid precipitation or seawater. As the iron corrodes, the porous graphite (soft carbon) corrosion residue is impregnated with insoluble corrosion products. As a result, the cast-iron element retains its appearance and shape but is weakened structurally. Graphitization occurs when cast iron is left unpainted for long periods or where caulked joints have failed and acidic rainwater has corroded pieces from the backside. Testing and identification of graphitization is accomplished by scraping through the surface with a knife to reveal the crumbling of the iron beneath. Where extensive graphitization has occurred, usually the only solution is replacement of the damaged element.

Castings may also be fractured or flawed as a result of imperfections in the original manufacturing process, such as air holes, cracks, and cinders, or cold shuts (caused by the "freezing" of the surface of the molten iron during casting because of improper or interrupted pouring). Brittleness is another problem occasionally found in old cast-iron elements. It may be a result of excessive phosphorus in the iron or of chilling during the casting process.

RESTORATION OF CAST IRON

Before establishing the appropriate treatment for cast-iron building elements, the historical and architectural significance of the elements and their present condition should be evaluated. If the work involves more than routine maintenance, a qualified professional should be engaged to document existing conditions and provide detailed recommendations for restoration. Through this process, the significance and condition of the cast iron can be evaluated and appropriate treatments proposed.

The nature and extent of the problems with the cast-iron elements must be well understood before proceeding with work. If the problems are minor, such as surface corrosion, flaking paint, and failed caulking, the property owner may be able to undertake the repairs by working directly with a knowledgeable contractor. If there are major problems or extensive damage to the cast iron, it is best to secure the services of an architect or conservator who specializes in the conservation of historic buildings. Depending on the scope of work, contract documents can range from an outline specification to complete working drawings with annotated photographs and specifications.

To thoroughly assess the condition of the ironwork, a close physical inspection must be undertaken of every section of the iron construction, including bolts, fasteners, and brackets. Typically, scaffolding or a mechanical lift is employed for close inspection of a cast-iron façade or other large structure. Removal of select areas of paint may be the only means to determine the exact conditions of connections, metal fasteners, and intersections or crevices that might trap water.

An investigation of load-bearing elements, such as columns and beams, will establish whether these components are performing as they were originally designed or if the stress patterns have been redistributed. Areas that are abnormally stressed must be examined to ascertain whether they have suffered damage or have been displaced. Damage to a primary structural member must be identified and evaluated.

Whether minor or major work is required, it is preferable to retain and repair rather than to replace historic ironwork. All repairs and restoration work should be reversible, when possible, so that modifications or treatments that may turn out to be harmful to the long-term preservation of the iron can be corrected with the least amount of damage to the historic elements.

Cleaning and Paint Removal

When there is extensive failure of the protective coating and/or when heavy corrosion exists, the rust and most or all of the paint must be removed to prepare the surfaces for new protective coatings. The techniques available range from physical processes, such as wire-brushing and grit-blasting, to flame-cleaning and chemical methods. The selection of an appropriate technique depends on how much paint failure and corrosion has occurred, the fineness of the surface detailing, and the type of new protective coating to be applied. Local environmental regulations may restrict the options for cleaning and paint removal methods, as well as the disposal of materials.

Many of these techniques are potentially dangerous and should be carried out only by experienced and qualified workers wearing proper eye protection and protective clothing, and implementing other workplace safety precautions. Before selecting a process, test panels should be prepared on the iron to be cleaned to determine the relative effectiveness of various techniques. The cleaning process will most likely expose additional coating defects, cracks, and corrosion that have not been obvious before.

There are a number of techniques that can be used to remove paint and corrosion from cast iron. Hand-scraping, chipping, and wire-brushing are the most common and least expensive methods of removing paint and light rust from cast iron. However, they do not remove all corrosion or paint as effectively as other methods. Experienced craftspeople should carry out the work to reduce the likelihood that surfaces may be scored or fragile detail damaged.

Low-pressure grit-blasting (commonly called abrasive cleaning or sandblasting) is often the most effective approach to removing excessive paint buildup or substantial corrosion. Grit-blasting is fast, thorough, and economical, and it allows the iron to be cleaned in place. The aggregate can be iron slag or sand (copper slag should not be used on iron because of the potential for electrolytic reactions). Some sharpness in the aggregate is beneficial in that it gives the metal surface a "tooth" that will result in better paint adhesion. The use of a very sharp or hard aggregate and/or excessively high pressure (over 100 pounds per square inch) is unnecessary and should be avoided. Adjacent materials, such as brick, stone, wood, and glass, must be protected to prevent damage. Some local building codes and environmental authorities prohibit or limit dry sandblasting because of the problem of airborne dust.

Wet sandblasting is more problematic than dry sandblasting for cleaning cast iron because the water will cause instantaneous surface rusting and will penetrate deep into open joints. Therefore, it is generally not considered an effective technique. And although wet sandblasting reduces the amount of airborne dust when removing a heavy paint buildup, disposal of effluent containing lead or other toxic substances is restricted by environmental regulations in most areas.

Flame-cleaning of rust from metal with a special multiflame head oxyacetylene torch requires specially skilled operators, and is expensive and potentially dangerous. However, it can be very effective on lightly to moderately corroded iron. Wire-brushing is usually necessary to finish preparing the surface after flame-cleaning.

Chemical rust removal, by acid pickling, is an effective method of removing rust from iron elements that can be easily removed and taken to a shop for submerging in vats of dilute phosphoric or sulfuric acid. This method does not damage the surface of iron, providing that the iron is neutralized to pH level 7 after cleaning. Other chemical rust removal agents include ammonium citrate, oxalic acid, or hydrochloric acid-based products.

Chemical paint removal using alkaline compounds, such as methylene chloride or potassium hydroxide, can be an effective alternative to abrasive blasting for removal of heavy paint buildup.

These agents are often available as slow-acting gels or pastes. Because they can cause burns, protective clothing and eye protection must be worn. Chemicals applied to a nonwatertight façade can seep through crevices and holes, resulting in damage to the building's interior finishes and corrosion to the backside of the iron components. If not thoroughly neutralized, residual traces of cleaning compounds on the surface of the iron can cause paint failures in the future. For these reasons, field application of alkaline paint removers and acidic cleaners is not generally recommended.

Following any of these methods of cleaning and paint removal, the newly cleaned iron should be painted immediately with a corrosion-inhibiting primer before new rust begins to form. This time period may vary from minutes to hours depending on environmental conditions. If priming is delayed, any surface rust that has developed should be removed with a clean wire brush just before priming, because the rust prevents good bonding between the primer and the cast-iron surface, and prevents the primer from completely filling the pores of the metal.

Painting and Coating Systems

The most common and effective way to preserve architectural cast iron is to maintain a protective coating of paint on the metal. Paint can also be decorative, where historically appropriate.

Before removing paint from historic architectural cast iron, a microscopic analysis of samples of the historic paint sequencing is recommended. Called paint seriation analysis, this process must be carried out by an experienced architectural conservator. The analysis will identify the historic paint colors and other conditions, such as whether the paint was matte or gloss, whether sand was added to the paint for texture, and whether the building was polychromed or marbleized. Traditionally, many cast-iron elements were painted to resemble other materials, such as limestone or sandstone. Occasionally, features were faux-painted so that the iron appeared to be veined marble.

Thorough surface preparation is necessary for the adhesion of new protective coatings. All loose, flaking, and deteriorated paint must be removed from the iron, as well as dirt and mud, water-soluble salts, oil, and grease. Old paint that is tightly adhered may be left on the surface of the iron if it is compatible with the proposed coatings. The retention of old paint also preserves the historic paint sequence of the building and avoids the hazards of removal and disposal of old lead paint. It is advisable to consult manufacturer's specifications or technical representatives to ensure compatibility between the surface conditions, primer and finish coats, and application methods.

For the paint to adhere properly, the metal surfaces must be absolutely dry before painting. Unless the paint selected is specifically designed for exceptional conditions, painting should not take place when the temperature is expected to fall below 50 degrees Fahrenheit within 24 hours or when the relative humidity is above 80 percent; paint should not be applied when there is fog, mist, or rain in the air. Poorly prepared surfaces will cause the failure of even the best paints, while even moderately priced paints can be effective if applied over well-prepared surfaces.

Selection of Paints and Coatings

The types of paints available for protecting iron have changed dramatically in recent years because of federal, state, and local regulations that prohibit or restrict the manufacture and use of products containing toxic substances such as lead and zinc chromate, as well as volatile organic compounds and substances (VOC or VOS). Availability of paint types varies from state to state, and manufacturers continue to change product formulations to comply with new regulations.

Traditionally, red lead has been used as an anticorrosive pigment for priming iron. Red lead has a strong affinity for linseed oil and forms lead soaps, which become a tough and elastic film impervious to water that is highly effective as a protective coating for iron. At least two slow-drying linseed oil-based finish coats have traditionally been used over a red lead primer, and this combination is effective on old or partially deteriorated surfaces. Today, in most areas, the use of paints containing lead is restricted, except for some commercial and industrial purposes.

Currently, alkyd paints have largely replaced lead-containing linseed-oil paints. They dry faster than oil paint, with a thinner film, but they do not protect the metal as long. Alkyd rust-inhibitive primers contain pigments such as iron oxide, zinc oxide, and zinc phosphate. These primers are suitable for previously painted surfaces cleaned by hand tools. At least two coats of primer should be applied, followed by alkyd enamel finish coats.

Latex and other water-based paints are not recommended for use as primers on cast iron because they cause immediate oxidation if applied on bare metal. Vinyl acrylic latex or acrylic latex paints may be used as finish coats over alkyd rust-inhibitive primers, but if the primer coats are imperfectly applied or are damaged, the latex paint will cause oxidation of the iron. Therefore, alkyd finish coats are recommended.

High-performance coatings, such as zinc-rich primers containing zinc dust, and modern epoxy coatings, can be used on cast iron to provide longer-lasting protection. These coatings typically require highly cleaned surfaces and special application conditions, which can be difficult to achieve in the field on large buildings. These coatings are used most effectively on elements that have been removed to a shop or on newly cast iron.

One particularly effective system has been first to coat commercially blast-cleaned iron with a zinc-rich primer, followed by an epoxy base coat and two urethane finish coats. Some epoxy coatings can be used as primers on clean metal or applied to previously painted surfaces in sound condition. Epoxies are particularly susceptible to degradation under ultraviolet radiation and must be protected by finish coats that are more resistant. There have been problems with shop-applied epoxy paints where the coatings have been nicked prior to installation. Field touching-up of epoxy paints is very difficult, if not impossible. Damaged epoxy base coats are a concern since iron exposed by imperfections in the base coat will be more likely to rust, and more frequent maintenance will be required.

A key consideration in selection of coatings is the variety of conditions on existing and new materials on a particular building or structure. One primer may be needed for surfaces with existing paint; another for newly cast, chemically stripped, or blast-cleaned cast iron; and a third for flashings or substitute materials. All three primers must be followed by compatible finish coats.

Application Methods

Brushing is the traditional and most effective technique for applying paint to cast iron. It provides good contact between the paint and iron, as well as the effective filling of pits, cracks, and other blemishes in the metal. The use of spray guns to apply paint is economical, but does not always produce adequate and uniform coverage. For best results, airless sprayers should be used by skilled operators. To fully cover fine detailing and reach recesses, spraying of the primer coat, used in conjunction with brushing, may be effective.

Rollers should never be used for primer coat applications on metal, and are effective for subsequent coats only on large, flat areas. The appearance of spray-applied and roller-applied finish coats is not historically appropriate and should be avoided on areas, such as storefronts, that are viewed at close range.

Caulking, Patching, and Mechanical Repairs

Most architectural cast iron is made of many small castings assembled by bolts or screws. Joints between pieces are caulked to prevent water from seeping in and causing rusting from the inside out. Historically, the seams were often caulked with white lead paste and sometimes backed with cotton or hemp rope; even the bolt and screw heads were caulked to protect them from the elements and to hide them from view. Although old caulking is sometimes found in good condition, it is typically crumbled from weathering, cracked from structural settlement, or destroyed by mechanical cleaning. It is essential to replace deteriorated caulking to prevent water penetration. For good adhesion and performance, an architectural-grade polyurethane sealant or traditional white lead paste is preferred.

Water that penetrates the hollow parts of a cast-iron architectural element causes rust that may streak down over other architectural elements. The water may freeze, causing the cast iron to crack. Cracks reduce the strength of the total cast-iron assembly and provide another point of entry for water. Thus, it is important that cracks be made weathertight by using caulks or fillers, depending on the width of the crack.

Filler compounds containing iron particles in an epoxy resin binder can be used to patch superficial, nonstructural cracks and small defects in cast iron. The thermal expansion rate of epoxy resin alone is different from that of iron, requiring the addition of iron particles to ensure compatibility and to control shrinkage. Although the repaired piece of metal does not have the same strength as a homogeneous piece of iron, epoxy-repaired members do have some strength. Polyester-based putties, such as those used on auto bodies, are also acceptable fillers for small holes. (Fig. 9.4)

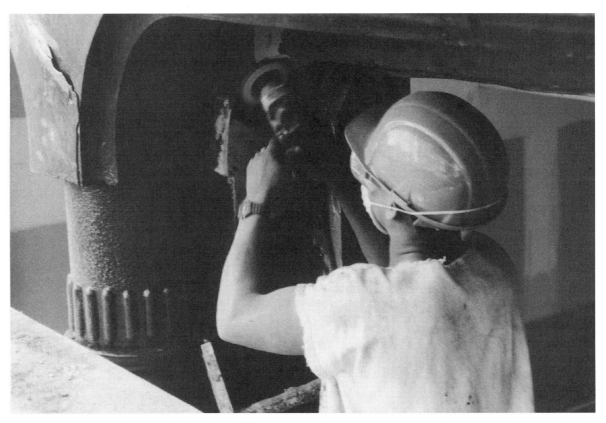

FIGURE. 9.4. *After filling areas with an epoxy resin patching material, the surface is ground in preparation for painting.* Raymond M. Pepi, President, Building Conservation Associates, Inc.

In rare instances, major cracks can be repaired by brazing or welding with special nickel-alloy welding rods. Brazing or welding of cast iron is very difficult to carry out in the field and should be undertaken only by very experienced welders.

In some cases, mechanical repairs can be made to cast iron using iron bars and screws or bolts. In extreme cases, deteriorated cast iron can be cut out and new cast iron spliced in place by welding or brazing. However, it is frequently less expensive to replace a deteriorated cast-iron section with a new casting rather than to splice or reinforce it. Cast-iron structural elements that have failed must either be reinforced with iron and steel or replaced entirely.

A wobbly cast-iron element can often be fixed by tightening all bolts and screws. Screws with stripped threads and seriously rusted bolts must be replaced. To compensate for corroded metal around the bolt or screw holes, new stainless steel bolts or screws with a larger diameter need to be used. In extreme cases, new holes may need to be tapped.

The internal voids of hollow iron elements should not be filled with concrete; it is an inappropriate treatment that causes further problems. As the concrete cures, it shrinks, leaving a space between the concrete and cast iron. Water penetrating this space does not evaporate quickly, thus promoting further rusting. The corrosion of the iron is further accelerated by the alkaline nature of concrete. Where cast-iron elements have been previously filled with concrete, they need to be taken apart, the concrete and rust removed, and the interior surfaces primed and painted before the elements are reassembled.

Duplication and Replacement

The replacement of cast-iron components is often the only practical solution when such features are missing, severely corroded, or damaged beyond repair, or where repairs would be only marginally useful in extending the functional life of an iron element.

Sometimes it is possible to replace small, decorative nonstructural elements using intact sections of the original as a casting pattern. For large sections, new patterns of wood or plastic made slightly larger in size than the original will need to be made in order to compensate for the shrinkage of the iron during casting (cast iron shrinks approximately 1/8 inch per foot as it cools from a liquid into a solid). Occasionally, a matching replacement can be obtained from the existing catalogs of iron foundries, often at a cost comparable to substitute materials. Large elements and complex patterns will usually require the skills and facilities of a large firm that specializes in replication. (Fig. 9.5)

Dismantling and Assembly of Architectural Compounds

It is sometimes necessary to dismantle all or part of a cast-iron structure during restoration, if repairs cannot be successfully carried out in place. Dismantling should be done only under the direction of a preservation architect or architectural conservator who is experienced with historic cast iron. Extreme care must be taken since cast iron is very brittle, especially in cold weather.

Dismantling should follow the reverse order of construction, and reerection should occur, as much as possible, in the exact order of original assembly. Each piece should be numbered and keyed to record drawings. When work must be carried out in cold weather, care must be taken to avoid fracturing the iron elements by uneven heating of the members.

Both new castings and reused pieces should be painted with a shop-applied prime coat on all surfaces. All of the components should be laid out and preassembled to make sure that the alignment and fit are proper. Many of the original bolts, nuts, and screws may have to be replaced with similar fasteners of stainless steel.

After assembly at the site, joints that were historically caulked should be filled with an architectural-grade polyurethane sealant or the traditional white lead paste. White lead has the advantage of longevity, although its use is restricted in many areas.

FIGURE 9.5. *Replacement pieces of cast iron are used when deterioration is so severe that the piece is beyond restoration.* Stacy Albanese, Conservator, Building Conservation Associates, Inc.

Substitute Materials

In recent years, a number of metallic and nonmetallic materials have been used as substitutes for cast iron, although they were not used historically with cast iron. The most common have been cast aluminum, epoxies, reinforced polyester (fiberglass), and glass-fiber-reinforced concrete (GFRC). There are many factors to consider in using substitute materials. However, the basic principle is that every means of repairing deteriorating historic materials or replacing them with identical materials should be examined before turning to substitute materials.

Cast aluminum has been used recently as a substitute for cast iron, particularly for ornately detailed decorative elements. Aluminum is lighter in weight, more resistant to corrosion, and less brittle than cast iron. However, because it is dissimilar from iron, its placement in contact with or near cast iron may result in galvanic corrosion, and thus should be avoided. Special care must be taken in the application of paint coatings, particularly in the field. It is often difficult to achieve a durable coating after the original finish has failed. Because aluminum is weaker than iron, careful analysis is required whenever aluminum is being considered as a replacement material for structural cast-iron elements.

Epoxies are two-part, thermo-setting, resinous materials that can be molded into virtually any form. When molded, the epoxy is usually mixed with fillers such as sand, glass balloons, or stone chips. Since it is not a metal, galvanic corrosion does not occur. When mixed with sand or stone, it is often termed epoxy concrete or polymer concrete, a misnomer because no cementitious materials are included. Epoxies are particularly effective for replicating small, ornamental sections of cast iron. Epoxy elements must have a protective coating to shield them from ultraviolet degradation. They are also flammable and cannot be used as substitutes for structural cast-iron elements.

Reinforced polyester, commonly known as fiberglass, is often used as a lightweight substitute for historic materials, including cast iron, wood, and stone. In its most common form, fiberglass is a thin, rigid, laminate shell formed by pouring a polyester resin into a mold and then adding glass fibers for reinforcement. Like epoxies, fiberglass does not corrode, but is susceptible to ultraviolet degradation. Because of its rather flimsy nature, it cannot be used as a substitute for structural elements, cannot be assembled like cast iron, and usually requires a separate anchorage system. It is unsuitable for locations where it is susceptible to damage by impact. Fiberglass is also flammable.

Glass-fiber-reinforced concrete, known as GFRC, is similar to fiberglass except that a lightweight concrete is substituted for the resin. GFRC elements are generally fabricated as thin shell panels by spraying concrete into forms. Usually, a separate framing and anchorage system is required. GFRC elements are lightweight, inexpensive, and weather-resistant. Because GFRC has a low shrinkage coefficient, molds can be made directly from historic elements.

Maintenance

A successful maintenance program is the key to the long-term preservation of architectural cast iron. Regular inspections and accurate record-keeping are essential. Biannual inspections, occurring ideally in the spring and fall, include the identification of major problems, such as missing elements and fractures, as well as minor items such as failed caulking, damaged paint, and surface dirt.

Records should be kept in the form of a permanent maintenance log, which describes routine maintenance tasks and records the date a problem is first noted, when it is corrected, and the treatment method. Painting records are important for selecting compatible paints for touch-up and subsequent repainting. The location of the work and the type, manufacturer, and the color of the paint should be noted in the log. The same information also should be assembled and recorded for caulking.

Superficial dirt can be washed off well-painted and caulked cast iron with low-pressure water. Nonionic detergents may be used for the removal of heavy or tenacious dirt or stains, after testing to determine that they have no adverse effects on the painted surfaces. Thick grease deposits and residue can be removed by hand-scraping. Water and detergents or noncaustic degreasing agents can be used to clean off the residue. Before repainting, oil and grease must be removed so that new coatings will adhere properly.

The primary purpose of the maintenance program is to control corrosion. As soon as rusting is noted, it should be carefully removed and the protective coating of the iron renewed in the affected area. Replacement of deteriorated caulking and repair or replacement of failed flashings are also important preventive maintenance measures.

10

SHEET METAL

John G. Waite

HISTORICAL BACKGROUND

ALTHOUGH CAST IRON WAS THE architectural metal most widely used in historic building façades, other metals were used during the late 19th and early 20th centuries in the form of sheets that were fabricated into architectural elements. These metals include tinplate (tin applied to sheet iron or steel), terneplate (tin and lead alloy coating applied to sheet iron or steel), copper, zinc, and galvanized (zinc-coated) iron or steel. Sheet metal could easily be formed into a variety of shapes resembling stone, terra-cotta or cast iron; it was light in weight and was very economical compared with cast iron or masonry elements. For these reasons, sheet metal was commonly used for such nonload-bearing architectural elements as projecting cornices, lintels, sills, balustrades, and entire storefronts. (Fig. 10.1)

Some metals, such as copper, develop a protective coating when exposed to the atmosphere, while others, such as iron and zinc, require plating with a sacrificial metal coating or the application of a renewable organic coating such as paint for long-term protection. Copper is one of the most corrosion-resistant architectural metals; it is ductile, malleable, nonmagnetic, high in electrical and thermal conductivity, and is easily soldered. Copper is initially a bright reddish-brown in color, but when exposed to the atmosphere, it acquires a protective patina that turns from brown to black to green over a period of several decades. The patina is actually a thin, tough layer of corrosion that prevents deeper and deeper layers of corrosion. Therefore, even though copper corrodes, it is corrosion-resistant.

Copper was first rolled in the late 17th century in England. By the end of the 18th century, sheet copper was used for the roofing of some large American public buildings and houses; George Washington used sheet copper on Mount Vernon in the 1780s. With the introduction of sheet-metal-working machinery, copper was widely used by the end of the 19th century for decorative architectural elements. (Fig. 10.2)

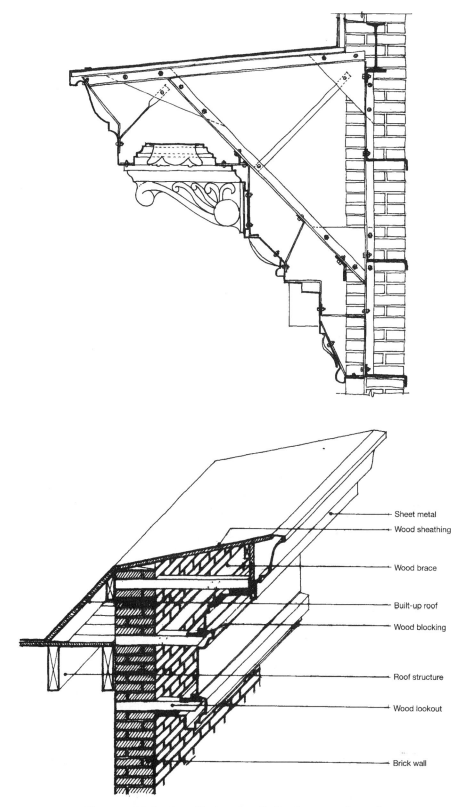

FIGURE 10.1. *Installation details for sheet metal cornices.*

FIGURE 10.2. *An example of sheet copper used for a decorative cornice.* Roger P. Lang, New York Landmarks Conservancy

Zinc is a medium-hard, bluish-white metal characterized by its brittleness and low strength. Zinc architectural elements are often mistaken for tin-plated or galvanized sheet iron. However, zinc is easily identified because it is softer than iron and is non-magnetic. Pure metallic zinc was first produced in commercial quantities in 1738 in England. Sheet zinc was first hot-rolled and patented in 1805. By the 1820s, sheet zinc was being imported into the United States from Belgium. By mid-century, its use for roofing was fairly widespread.

Iron is a gray-white metal, which in its pure form is relatively soft, tough, malleable, ductile, magnetic, and high in tensile strength. It oxidizes rapidly when exposed to a damp atmosphere and is readily attacked by most acids. Historically, iron in a number of alloy forms has been used for architectural purposes. When alloyed with small amounts of carbon (not more than 2 percent), steel is formed.

In the United States, iron was first rolled in Trenton, New Jersey; it was used to roof a house in Philadelphia about 1794. At first, sheet iron was coated with tin to resist corrosion. Later, terne, a mixture of tin and lead, was used. In 1837, the first patents were issued for galvanizing, a process for coating sheet iron with zinc. By 1839, galvanized sheet iron roofing was used in New York City. The first sheet iron cornices were constructed in 1834, and by the early 1840s, machines for forming cornices of sheet iron were in use.

DETERIORATION AND EVALUATION OF SHEET METAL

Deterioration is the breakdown of a material so that it loses its ability to fulfill the function for which it was intended. Usually associated with the breakdown of a material because of natural causes, it can also be caused directly or indirectly by humans. Although deterioration usually implies a chemical change, under some conditions, the change can be physical. (Fig. 10.3)

General Causes of Sheet Metal Deterioration

Corrosion. The major cause of the deterioration of architectural metals is corrosion. Often called oxidation, it is the chemical reaction of a metal with oxygen or other substances. Constantly undergoing change, metals exposed to the atmosphere, heat, moisture, pressure, or other agents, tend to transform from a pure state, such as iron and copper, to their natural ores, such as iron oxide and copper sulfide. The deterioration of metal architectural elements is a complex process because the types and degree of corrosion are affected by minor variations in environment, contact with other metals and materials, and the composition of the metal itself.

Metal architectural elements can also fail from purely physical causes such as abrasion, or a combination of physical and chemical attack, such as weathering and stress corrosion cracking.

Abrasion. Abrasion is the erosion of the metal caused by the impact of dirt, dust, sand, grit, rain, sleet, and hail, or by rubbing with another architectural element or human contact. Abrasives can also exacerbate corrosion by removing protective corrosion deposits from the metal surface.

FIGURE 10.3. *Deterioration of sheet metal-clad architectural element caused by inadequate structural support, resulting in open joints in metal cladding.* John F. Favazzo, New York Landmarks Conservancy

Fatigue. Fatigue is failure of a metal by the repeated application of cyclic stresses below the elastic limit—the greatest stress a metal can withstand without permanent deformation after removal of the load. It results from a gradual or progressive fracture of the crystals. Often it is caused by lack of provisions to accommodate thermal expansion and contraction. Often, the visible sign of this type of deterioration is open, or broken, joints between the metal sheets.

Fire. Fire can cause unprotected sheet metal elements to buckle or fall off buildings when their anchorage is lost.

Combined Attack. A metal architectural element subjected to the weather is exposed to various chemical and physical agents at one time. The result is a kind of synergism where the total effect is greater than the sum of the individual effects. For example, the rate of corrosion accelerates with increases of temperature, humidity, and surface deposits of salts, dirt, and pollution.

Deterioration of Specific Metals

In addition to the general types of deterioration, individual metals have peculiar qualities that lead to their breakdown and failure.

Copper. Copper is highly resistant to corrosion caused by the atmosphere or salt water. It combines with hydrogen sulfide and oxygen or sulfur dioxide to form a protective copper carbonate or copper sulfate patina, which resists further corrosion and generally does not change further in appearance. However, copper is attacked by alkalis, ammonia, and various sulfur compounds that can combine with water to form sulfuric acid. Some bituminous coatings, containing sulfur compounds, will attack copper, as will sulfate-reducing bacteria, which act as a catalyst for corrosion. Copper is also corroded by rainwater that has become acidic through contact with moss, lichen, algae, or wood shingles.

Copper is not very active galvanically and, therefore, is not usually subject to galvanic corrosion unless it is in contact with more noble metals, such as some stainless steels. However, if an electrolyte is present, the copper will act as a cathode and corrode other, more active, metals such as iron or steel.

Sheet copper is vulnerable to mechanical breakdown of the individual metal units caused by insufficient provisions for thermal expansion and contraction, inadequate sheet thickness, excessively large sheet size, improper fastenings, insufficient substructure, and erosion caused by particle abrasion or the velocity effect of aerated water. Excessive thermal stressing causes the copper and its protective patina to become friable; eventually, the metal may fatigue, resulting in bulges and cracks. Any sheet copper architectural element can fail from using the wrong temper or gauge of copper or from using fastenings that restrict free movement.

Because of its softness, copper is easily eroded by abrasive agents. It is also vulnerable to impact damage such as hail, and to fatigue and "inelastic deformation" as the result of wind damage. Further, the protective patina of sheet copper may be soluble in rain contaminated with dissolved chemicals. When the patina is washed away, fresh metal is exposed; it in turn corrodes, is dissolved, and washes away again. If the cycle is repeated many times, a significant loss of material can result. Severe pitting and obvious loss of material from corrosion are a good indication that the patina is not protective.

Zinc. Zinc is not resistant to acids or strong alkalis and is particularly vulnerable to corrosion by sulfur acids produced by the hydrogen sulfide and sulfur dioxide pollution in urban atmospheres. Zinc is also attacked by acids found in redwood, cedar, oak, and sweet chestnut, and can be corroded by plasters and cements, especially portland cements containing chlorides and sulfates. Condensation on the underside of zinc plates and ponded water on the exterior surface of zinc architectural ornament can also lead to corrosion. Zinc also deteriorates on contact with acidic rainwater runoff from roofs with wood shingles, moss, or lichen.

Although zinc develops a carbonate on its surface by exposure to the atmosphere and by the action of rainwater, the film is not dense or adherent enough to protect the zinc from continued attack. The carbonate becomes brittle and crusty and eventually splits, exposing fresh zinc for corrosion. Thermal movement of the zinc is also damaging to the carbonate film. In industrial atmospheres, the zinc carbonate film is broken down by the same acids that attack zinc. These acids convert the carbonate to zinc sulfate, which is water-soluble and washes away with rainwater, often staining adjacent building elements.

Zinc has a relatively high coefficient of thermal expansion and is therefore vulnerable to fatigue failure. Because zinc is relatively soft, it is also vulnerable to abrasion damage. And although zinc is not damaged by electrical contact with lead, galvanized iron and steel, tin, or aluminum, it is damaged by galvanic corrosion when it comes in electrical contact with copper and pure iron in a common electrolyte.

Flaking and peeling of the zinc coating is a problem with old, hot-dipped galvanized iron sheets. Because of the galvanizing techniques used, a thick, brittle coating of zinc was formed. This coating can peel and flake when the iron sheet is deformed—that is, folded and stamped—after the coating has been applied, exposing the iron sheet to corrosion.

Galvanized sheets and pure zinc sheets are also attacked by a type of corrosion known as white stain or white rust. Closely stacked sheets stored either in a warehouse or unprotected outdoors will be attacked if dampness and extreme temperatures occur. With the absence of oxygen and carbon dioxide between the sheets, the protective layer of zinc hydroxide is formed with resultant loss of metallic zinc. The corrosion then appears as a voluminous white powder. Perforation of the galvanized or zinc sheets can occur rapidly, causing significant damage.

Sheet Iron and Steel. When unprotected, sheet iron and steel oxidize rapidly when exposed to moisture and air. The oxidation of iron and steel is a highly destructive process. The product of this oxidation is rust, which initially consists of a mixture of ferrous and ferric hydroxides (FeO), and later becomes a hydrated ferric oxide ($Fe_2(OH)_3$) with some traces of a carbonate. The minimum relative humidity necessary to promote rusting is 65 percent, but this figure can be lower in the presence of pollutants. Once rust occurs, its porosity acts as a reservoir for any liquid present, which also tends to accelerate corrosion. If simple oxidation is not arrested, its rate will accelerate until the metal is completely destroyed.

Iron and steel are also corroded by seawater, salt air, acids, soils, gypsum plasters, magnesium oxychloride cements, ashes and clinkers, and some sulfur compounds. Corrosion is accelerated where architectural details provide pockets and crevices to catch and hold these corrosive agents.

Galvanic corrosion is an especially serious problem for sheet iron and steel. Galvanic corrosion will occur when the iron and steel are exposed to cupro-nickels, copper, lead, soft solder, and stainless steel.

Galvanized Iron and Steel. Galvanized ferrous metals can resist corrosion, but the level of resistance is dependent on the type and thickness of the protective zinc coating, the type and thickness of additional protective coatings, and the kind of corrosive environment to which they are exposed. Galvanized steel can generally be used in direct contact with most woods, excluding cedar, oak, sweet chestnut, and redwood, all of which produce acids. However, just the contact of any moist wood against the metal can cause an O_2 concentration cell. Galvanized iron and steel can be used with concrete, mortar, lead, tin, zinc, and aluminum. Galvanic corrosion occurs, however, when galvanized metal is in contact with any of the other metals. Like most types of iron and steel, galvanized steel is also corroded by acids and chemical fumes.

Tinplate and Terneplate. Throughout the 19th and into the early 20th century, the most common protective coatings for sheet iron and steel were tin or terne, a mixture of lead and tin. Called tinplate and terneplate, these iron and steel sheets were commonly used for roofing and wall cladding, as well as decorative architectural elements.

The tin and terneplatings on iron sheets are stable coatings that resist corrosion caused by oxygen, moisture, sulfur dioxide, and hydrogen sulfide, when properly protected. When exposed to the atmosphere, tin readily develops a thin film of stannic oxide, which helps resist corrosion. Although pure tin is mildly corroded by exposure to acids, marine atmospheres, and certain alkalis, tinplate roofing is generally very durable as long as the tin or terne coating maintains its integrity. Once the plating has been broken and the iron or steel is exposed to oxygen, the deterioration begins and is accelerated by the galvanic action between the tin and iron. This action protects the iron from corrosion but accelerates the deterioration of the tin, exposing more of the iron to be corroded.

Tin and terneplate roofing and flashing will deteriorate when in contact with copper; for instance, in gutters. Also, they can be corroded by asphaltic and bituminous roofing compounds and building paper, as well as by paints containing acids, bitumen, asphalt, or aluminum. Tinplate can corrode on the underside from water vapor condensation if the tin is not protected by a coating of paint and/or a nonacidic vapor barrier.

Stainless Steels. Stainless steels have a high resistance to heat, oxidation, and corrosion. Chromium and chromium-nickel stainless steels are among the few metals that remain substantially unaltered in appearance after being exposed to the atmosphere. Stainless steels resist corrosion from hydrogen sulfide and sulfur dioxide, and have good resistance to water and to some soils; thus, they often retain their natural finishes.

TREATMENT AND REPAIR OF SHEET METAL

The same process as described for cast iron should be used to determine the condition and significance of sheet metal elements. Once this process has been completed, appropriate methods and levels of treatment can be evaluated. Sheet metal elements are usually more fragile and vulnerable to damage than those of cast iron.

The most common practice of protecting architectural metals from corrosion is the application of organic coatings (paints). Generally, the success of the coating depends on surface preparation, type of primer and finish coatings, and the methods of application. Paints reduce corrosion by permitting only a sluggish movement of ions through the paint film lying between the metal and corrosive environment. Discussions on paint are expanded later.

Before painting, sheet metal elements usually need to be cleaned to remove products of corrosion and previous paint coatings. Most sheet metals used on historic buildings, with the possible exception of iron and steel, should not be cleaned mechanically because they are quite soft and/or thin and pliable, and they would be deformed or their surfaces abraded by such a process. It is usually preferable to clean these metals—copper, zinc, tinplate, and terneplate—with a chemical or thermal method. Commonly, using a noncorrosive chemical paint remover is the method of choice for cleaning sheet metal architectural elements.

Once the surface of the metal has been cleaned of all corrosion products (standards exist to determine the degree of cleaning), a primer coat consisting of a liquid vehicle and a corrosion-resisting pigment is applied. The primer should be applied as soon as possible after cleaning. When the primer is thoroughly dry, the finish coats, which generally consist of lacquers, varnishes (resins in solvent), enamels (pigmented varnishes), or special coatings, are applied.

Metal architectural elements that have deteriorated or failed because of corrosion or physical breakdown, especially fatigue or overloading, can sometimes be repaired by patching or reinforcing.

Patching

Patching requires mending, covering, or filling a deteriorated area with another piece of material. Depending on the type of metal and its location, the patch can be applied by soldering or by using mechanical connections, such as rivets. For example, a copper cornice with localized deterioration or damage may be patched with sheet copper that has been folded or pressed to match the design of the section of the cornice being patched. Often, patching refers to the repair of nonstructural architectural elements. (Fig. 10.4) To prevent galvanic corrosion, the patch material should be a very close match to the original material, or it should be insulated from the original metal with nonporous insulation.

Reinforcing

Reinforcing is the repair of a damaged or deteriorated element by supplementing it with new metal material. The new metal does not replace the deteriorated element, but is added to it so the old material can continue to serve its intended purpose.

FIGURE 10.4. *Sheet metal used to patch existing sheet metal is formed to match the design and contour of the area being patched. Care should be taken to avoid galvanic corrosion by patching with a metal that is compatible with the surrounding metal.* Raymond M. Pepi, President, Building Conservation Associates, Inc.

In some cases, such as opened joints, the repair can be made simply be resoldering the joint. In other situations, small holes or dents can be filled using polyester-based putties, such as those used on automobile bodies.

Replacement

When sheet metal architectural components are beyond repair or when the repairs are only marginally useful in extending the functional life of the member, replacement of the deteriorated element with the reproduction material is often the only practical solution. If the metal has deteriorated to a point where it has actually failed, duplication and replacement is the only course of action.

Where deteriorated sheet metal components are visually important to the building, they should be replaced with materials that duplicate the appearance of the old by matching the original material in composition, size, and configuration of details.

Copper

Copper is very durable and seldom needs maintenance, but it can be painted to prevent erosion. It can be difficult, however, to obtain a good bond between the copper and paint because grease and oil are rolled into the surface pores of the copper during manufacturing. Traditionally, lead-based paints were often used in the first or prime coat to obtain a good paint bond to the metal. The following instructions for cleaning and for obtaining a good paint bond are from a 1956 edition of Kidder-Parker.[1]

1. The surface must be thoroughly cleaned and roughened using a solution of 4 ounces copper sulfate to 1/2-gallon lukewarm water with 1/8-ounce nitric acid.
2. The first coat of paint is to consist of 15 pounds red lead to 1 gallon raw linseed oil, with not more than 1/2-pint oil dryer.
3. The final two coats of paint are to consist of 15 pounds white lead to 1 gallon raw linseed oil and not more than 5 percent oil dryer and color pigments.

Alkyd resin paints specially formulated for copper use with the appropriate primer are now usually substituted for the lead-base paint, but alkyd resin paints do not provide as good protection against erosion and the metal must be repainted more often.

Because the traditional red and white lead paints are now considered to be health hazards, high-performance coating systems, such as epoxy primer and urethane finish coats, are now used in place of the traditional red lead and linseed oil paint. (Note: The water runoff from roofs with copper valleys painted with lead-based paint is just as harmful, if ingested, as water from lead or lead-coated copper roofs.

There are some cases where a natural or unpainted copper color is desirable; hence, a clear coating is used. After the copper elements are completely cleaned of flux, dirt, and oxide by a recommended process of abrasion, they can be protected by a lacquer or Incralac coating. Incralac contains an acrylic resin, a chelating agent (Benztriazole), and a leveling agent in toluene or butyl acetate. The application of three separate coats should build up an optimal protective coating of more than 0.001 inches in thickness on the surface. If lacquer or Incralac is used to coat copper, the copper will retain its original color for a number of years; the natural protective patina will not form, except where the coating is broken or worn away. In addition to lacquer, wax coatings may also be used to protect the copper.

When copper architectural elements deteriorate, they should be examined by a specialist to determine if they can be salvaged. If this is not possible, the damaged element should be replaced with new copper of the same weight, configuration, and temper or hardness. Fatigue damage should never be repaired using soldered patches or soft solder (a lead-tin alloy) to fill stress cracks; this solder has a different coefficient of expansion than the copper and will eventually break away. Solder is inherently a weak alloy and should be used only to create watertight joints, not where tensile or compressive strength is needed. However, solder does provide some strength in connecting sheets of copper in "weights" less than 20 ounces. To connect thicker sheets, over 20 ounces, copper rivets must be used. All solder used for copper, either for repair or new installations, should be composed of 50 percent pig lead and 50 percent block tin, and should be applied using a noncorrosive rosin flux. Copper can be welded if the sheets are of sufficient thickness.

Where new sheets of copper are used to repair an existing copper architectural component, the maximum length of the sheets should be 9 feet. Adequate provisions should be made for thermal expansion and contraction within the repaired area, and all fastenings should use copper cleats held with either copper nails or brass screws. Copper roofing sheets should be separated from the wooden sheathing by rosin building paper to allow free movement of the sheets.

Zinc and Zinc Coatings

It is difficult to carry out piecemeal *in situ* repairs to pure zinc architectural elements, except under unusual circumstances. Where repairs can be made, solder with a composition of 50 percent tin and 50 percent lead or 60 percent tin and 40 percent lead (antimony-free) is used. A hydrochloric acid flux should be used, but it should be remembered that the flux can dissolve zinc. The excess flux must be rinsed immediately after soldering. Where the zinc is badly eroded, the only practical solution may be to replace the damaged section with new material.

When used with redwood, cedar, oak, or sweet chestnut, galvanized steel or iron should be protected from the acids in the wood by a bituminous paint applied to the exposed surfaces. Even though galvanized iron and steel can be painted, preliminary surface treatments may be necessary. The metallic surface should be allowed to weather before painting (usually about six months); however, it should not weather until rust appears. After weathering, the surface should be wiped with a clean cloth and mineral spirits, not hydrochloric acid, muriatic acid, or vinegar (as recommended by some old paint references), and painted with a specially formulated primer for galvanized iron, followed by two finish coats of a compatible oil-based paint.

If old galvanized sheeting has begun to rust, it should be treated with zinc oxide and flaky aluminum prime coats followed by a finish coat containing flaky aluminum and flaky micaceous iron-ore pigments. Rusting may also be arrested by the application of a zinc-rich paint after the rust has substantially been removed.

In some cases where the galvanized coating has been scraped or worn away, it may be necessary to recoat the sheet with zinc. The surface of the iron must be thoroughly cleaned, and one of the galvanizing processes discussed previously must be used. This must be done under controlled conditions in a shop and not *in situ*. When corrosion is not too severe, the surface can be cleaned and painted in place to prolong the life of the member. All corrosion, rust, and loose paint must be removed before painting. In other cases, it may be necessary to reproduce severely deteriorated or lost elements. In some situations, often for economic reasons, reinforced polyester, commonly known as fiberglass, has been used for reproduction of missing cornices and other sheet metal details.

Sheet Iron and Steel

Sheet iron and steel architectural components are most commonly protected from corrosion by paints. The paints most suitable for use on sheet iron and steel are the same as those recommended for cast iron. A discussion of these paints, along with cleaning methods, is located in Chapter 9, Cast Iron. For sheet metals, hand-scraping, wire-brushing, and chemical removers are the most common cleaning techniques. In some instances, low-pressure, dry, abrasive cleaning has been used with success. However, this technique should only be undertaken by a highly skilled and experienced technician because of the damage that could be done to the thin metal.

Techniques for repairing damaged tinplate or terneplate range from small localized patches to wholesale material replacement. If a joint in tinplate sheeting opens up, or a nail head pops up and punctures the tinplate, it should be repaired by cleaning and resoldering using a solder of 50 percent pig lead and 50 percent block tin applied with a rosin flux. Tinplate sheets should be fastened using only tinplate cleats and galvanized iron or steel nails. Copper alloy cleats and nails should not be used because of the potential for galvanic corrosion.

Priming and Painting. Priming and painting are mandatory; and for optimum protection, both sides (not just the exposed face) of the new tin or terneplate should be shop-coated with one coat and preferably two coats of an appropriate primer, such as linseed oil, iron oxide primer. Although seldom done, it is a good idea to apply a coat of compatible, high-gloss oil-based finish paint prior to installation as an added measure of protection, especially for the underside.

A finish coat should be applied immediately after installation, followed by another in two weeks. Finish coat paint used on tin roofs should employ only "metallic brown" (another name for iron oxide), "Venetian red" (ferric oxide, calcium carbonate, and ferrous sulfate), or red iron oxide (ferric oxide) pigments. The red lead pigments used in the past to provide very effective protection in the prime coat are now seldom used because it has been found that they constitute a serious health hazard. They have largely been replaced by alkyd-based iron oxide primers. Graphite and asphaltic base paints should not be used in tinplate or terneplate because they can encourage corrosion.

Replacement. Replacement of tinplate or terneplate sheets that have rusted through may be the only practical preservation solution. Damaged sections should be removed

FIGURE 10.5. *This sheet metal façade in Rytown, Ottawa, Canada, was originally mounted on a wood frame house. When the house was demolished, the façade was removed and hung on this stone wall like a piece of sculpture.* John G. Waite

and replaced with new materials of similar composition, configuration, and construction. Materials other than tinplate or terneplate should not be used to patch tinplate because galvanic corrosion will occur. However, if all of the tinplate must be replaced, it may be desirable to replace the old tinplate or terneplate with units of terne-coated stainless steel because this material is more durable and easier to maintain than tinplate. Although more expensive than terne-coated steel in initial cost, terne-coated stainless steel lasts longer and costs less to maintain if it is not painted.

If the new material is not applied using appropriate methods, its appearance will not duplicate that of a tinplate roof. Many sheet metal workers have a tendency to apply solder freely to the joints over the surface of the sheet material, resulting in a rough seam that may be an inch or more in width. These joints contrast greatly with historic tinplate seams where often no solder was visible on the surface of the metal. Also, 28-gauge terne-coated stainless steel, the thinnest, readily available gauge, is considerably thicker than historic tinplate, resulting in bends that are not as crisp or sharp.

Historically, tinplate seams were not often soldered. Instead, they either were installed dry, as was the case with the tin roofs designed by Thomas Jefferson, or the seams were filled with white lead paste. Today, white lead paste is difficult to obtain and constitutes a health hazard. Consequently, modern sealants are often used to fill the joints.

NOTES

1. Frank Kidder and Harry Parker, *Kidder-Parker Architects' and Builders' Handbook*, 18th ed. (New York, 1956), 2001.

11

WOOD

Contributions by Martin E. Weaver and John Leeke

HISTORICAL BACKGROUND

WOOD WAS ONE OF THE EARLIEST building materials and is still one of the most common. It has always been especially important in the United States where large virgin forests covered much of the land through the 19th century. Although wood has been used for both the structure and cladding of many buildings, its use on the façades of buildings of more than several stories has always been limited. The most fundamental reason for this limited use is its flammability. Most woods also require more frequent maintenance than do the masonry materials commonly used on building façades.

On the façades of multistory buildings built in the late 19th and first half of the 20th centuries, the most common use of exposed wood was for window frames and sash. In some instances, wood was also used for architectural ornament such as projecting cornices. In both cases, the wood was painted for protection. (Fig. 11.1)

During this period, too, wood was often used as framing to form concealed supports for projecting sheet metal elements. Wood lookouts and bracing for these elements were often embedded in masonry walls. Wood used for concealed supports was usually left uncoated.

PROPERTIES

The general properties of wood are well known. Among its positive qualities are its tensile and compressive strength, its flexibility, and the ease with which it can be worked. Among its negative aspects are its susceptibility to attack by insects, molds, and fungi; to cracking and weathering; and to destruction by fire. Nevertheless, some woods are nat-

FIGURE 11.1. *Wood is a material commonly used for projections and ornament, as well as moveable elements such as window sash.* James V. Banta, New York Landmarks Conservancy

urally resistant to rot and insect infestation, and it is possible to treat wood with preservatives and fire retardants to overcome its limitations.

The properties of wood vary considerably; it is not a uniform material even when it is cut from the same tree. As trees grow, two layers of wood are formed each year: a layer of soft porous wood called earlywood, and a layer of harder, denser wood termed latewood. Together, these layers make up the annual rings, which record the tree's age and its rate of growth. Narrower rings indicate slower growth. The number of rings per inch is one measure of wood quality; wood with more rings per inch is generally denser, stronger, and naturally more decay-resistant. Another indication of quality is the position of the wood in the cross-section of the log. In a small tree, the entire stem conducts sap to its branches. As the tree grows, not all of the wood is required to conduct the sap; the wood near the perimeter of the trunk, called sapwood, continues to serve that function. The wood in the center, called heartwood, having ceased to conduct sap, develops materials called extractives, which provide heartwoods with resistance to decay-causing fungi, increase their density, and make them somewhat more stable in changing moisture conditions. Thus, heartwoods from slow-growth trees are generally superior for use on building exteriors.

Although heartwood from slow-growth trees was readily available from America's virgin forests, most wood used today is from second- and third-growth stands. This wood, which has grown much more quickly than that of the original forests, has wider growth rings and less heartwood. It is not as strong or as decay-resistant as the wood cut in previous centuries.

The manner in which the lumber is sawn from a tree also affects its properties. Most common lumber, called flat-grain, is flat-sawn from the log. On the ends of a flat-grain board, the characteristic curving annual rings are roughly parallel to the faces of the board. Some lumber, called vertical-grain or edge-grain, is quarter-sawn or rift-sawn from the log so that the annual rings pass directly from one face of the board to the other. Vertical-grain wood performs better than flat-grain wood in façade applications. The vertical-grain board expands and contracts less in width with changes in moisture content. It also holds paint better. The paint film on a vertical-grain board suffers less stress than that on a flat-grain board because the wood moves less. In addition, the paint soaks in and adheres well to the porous earlywood and bridges over the denser latewood where adhesion is poor. On vertical-grain wood, the bridge is shorter and stronger than the bridge on flat-grain wood.

Because the wood used on old buildings was often rift-sawn or quarter-sawn from the heartwood of virgin timber, it is frequently superior to the wood generally available today. Thus, it is usually preferable to retain as much of the existing wood as possible. The wood in historic window sash, for example, is almost always of higher quality than the wood that would be used in replacement sash, making it wiser for the long-term preservation of the building to restore the existing sash rather than to replace them. Where existing wood cannot be saved, it is often possible to find old wood that has been salvaged from dismantled buildings or reclaimed from the bottoms of rivers or swamps.

Where it is determined necessary to use new wood to replace existing façade components, the best-quality seasoned wood with a maximum moisture content of 19 percent should be used.

EVALUATION AND ANALYSIS OF WOOD

Evaluation of Condition

Wood used for façade components is vulnerable to fire. Wood that has not been destroyed in this manner may have decayed. Deteriorated wood in window frames or sash may simply be unsightly. If the decay has progressed further, water may have entered the wall and damaged the masonry or other building components. Deterioration of wood used as supports for sheet metal work may lead eventually to structural failure, allowing elements to fall.

DETERIORATION OF WOOD BUILDING ELEMENTS

Coating Failure

Almost all exposed wood on urban buildings was originally covered by a protective coating. If the coating has failed, water may have entered the wood and decay may have begun. The coating may have failed for several reasons: it may not have been a good choice in the first place; it may have created a vapor barrier so that any water entering and trying to escape was trapped and caused a loss of adhesion; it may have been applied under improper conditions, that is, the wood may have been wet or too hot or too cold. The material used in the finish coats may not have been compatible with that used in the prime coat. Even if the coating was applied properly, it may have deteriorated because it was abraded, attacked by chemicals in the air, or weakened by ultraviolet rays. Coatings deteriorate over time and if not replaced, may deteriorate so completely that the wood itself is exposed to the elements.

Decay

Wood that is soft, spongy, crumbling, and cracked both with and across the grain is probably the victim of decay. (Fig. 11.2) Decay, or rot as it is also known, is caused by wood-destroying fungi, which feed on woody tissue. The fungi digest the wood materials by secreting enzymes, boring their way through the cell walls in the process. The major wood-destroying fungi can be classified by the appearance of the wood after it has been

FIGURE 11.2. *Wood decay is evident in soft, crumbly, or cracked areas of this window and trim.* John H. Stahl, Stahl Restorations

attacked. Thus, brown rots consume celluloses and leave lignin, which colors the remaining wood dark brown and often leaves it broken up into small cubes. White rots attack both the celluloses and the lignin leaving the wood whitish and with loose bundles of soft, punky fibers.

In order for decay to develop in wood, which serves as the nutrient source for the organism, three conditions are necessary. First, fungi require suitable temperatures, usually between 50 and 90 degrees Fahrenheit. Second, they require a small quantity of air. Third, they require sufficient moisture. Wood that is under water will not decay because there is no air to support the fungi. Wood that is maintained at a 20 percent moisture content or less is usually safe from fungal attack. Most decay occurs in wood that has a moisture content above the fiber saturation point.

Whether a piece of wood is readily susceptible or relatively resistant to decay depends on the species of wood and whether it came from the normally durable heart of the tree or from the nondurable outer layers of sapwood. Hardness and strength may have little to do with resistance to decay.

Certain tropical species such as teak and mahogany from which window frames and sash were often made are highly resistant to decay. Species from more temperate climates including cypress, redwood, walnut, white oak, and locust are durable and relatively resistant to decay. Spruce, red oak, birch, and poplar, for example, are liable to decay. Decay resistance, when it exists, is due to the presence in the heartwood of natural chemical substances called extractives.

Failure of Fastenings

Wood support members may fail because the fasteners failed. If the fastenings were of ferrous metal, for example, they may have rusted so extensively that they could no longer resist the load to which they were subjected.

REPAIR OF WOOD

Wood elements on façades of tall buildings are usually window frames, sash, and trim, but can include ornamental elements. They may require renewal of protective coatings or either minor or major repairs. Minor repairs include patching or replacing deteriorated coatings and filling small holes. Major repairs can include inserting small patches called dutchmen, or even replacing individual pieces of wood.

Protective Coatings

Originally wood elements on building façades were painted for protection. If the building has been properly maintained, the paint will have been renewed many times. If the paint has failed or is failing, it should be replaced after the surface has been properly prepared.

The coating on any surface painted before the third quarter of the 20th century may contain lead, which is highly toxic to humans and animals in relatively small concentrations. Lead can be absorbed through the skin, and lead dust and vapors can be inhaled. If such coatings are to be disturbed by scraping, sanding, or other means, they should be tested for the presence of lead. Coatings testing positive for lead should be handled following all regulations governing the removal and disposal of lead paint and all other precautions required to ensure that the lead will not be a hazard to persons or to the environment.

Surface Preparation. Proper preparation is the key to successful repainting and can extend the life of coatings by years. Usually, exterior wood surfaces in metropolitan areas have dirt deposits on them. The deposits are best washed off with clean water and detergent, then rinsed thoroughly and left to dry. All loose paint must be thoroughly scraped off. Knots, pitch or resin streaks, and sappy spots should be touched up with recommended primer. All areas of remaining paint should be lightly sanded to remove gloss, and all sanding dust should be removed using a cloth slightly dampened with paint solvent. Then the base coat should be applied. Following the base coat, nail holes, cracks, and other defects should be filled with wood putty designed specifically for exterior use and tinted to match the color of the finish.

Painting. The new wood coatings should be selected from the best-quality trade products of a single manufacturer and should be part of a "paint system" that includes primers and finish coats. Care should be taken to select coatings appropriate for the conditions present and for application over the underlying original paint types; some coatings might not be compatible with the existing paint. Each new coating should be applied precisely according to the manufacturer's instructions; requirements for temperature, humidity, and other conditions during application should be met explicitly. All wood exposed on the exterior of a building should receive a primer and two finish coats.

Minor Repair

Small Patches and Consolidation. Areas where the wood has become soft and crumbling or friable, but maintains its original profile may be consolidated. Small areas where the wood has rotted or broken away may be patched to restore the original surface planes and profiles. Several systems based on synthetic resins have been specifically designed for wood consolidation and patching. These systems, which typically include not only two-part epoxy resins, but also fillers, plasticizers, extenders, and types of reinforcement, have been widely used to repair window frames, sash, and wooden ornament. However, the expense of these materials usually limits their practical use to relatively small areas. (Fig. 11.3)

All coatings should be removed from areas of wood to be consolidated and patched, and the members should be dry. Small holes should be drilled through the areas of deteriorated wood to be consolidated, extending slightly into the surrounding sound wood to ensure that the consolidant will thoroughly penetrate the deteriorated areas. The resins and auxiliary materials should be handled, mixed, and applied strictly as directed by the manufacturer, because improper proportioning or mixing can result in failure. Particular attention should be paid to health and safety instructions because many of the synthetic resins and their catalysts may cause allergic reactions and other health problems.

FIGURE 11.3. *Rotten and missing areas of wooden members may be repaired using epoxy consolidation and patching.* John H. Stahl, Stahl Restorations

Note that the resins do not necessarily kill fungi or insects, and, therefore, attacks by these pests may require prior treatment in which case, care must then be taken to ensure that the pesticides are compatible with the resins and other repair materials, and vice versa.

Major Repair

Major repair of wood elements includes installation of dutchmen—sections of new wood that are inserted into existing members—and replacement of individual wood elements.

Dutchmen. In preparation for a dutchman, all deteriorated wood must be removed, and the sides of the hole cut square. A dutchman of wood that matches, or is at least compatible with, the original must be cut to fit the hole, leaving just sufficient clearance for glue joints. The grain of the new piece should run in the same direction as that of the original member so that they will expand and contract in the same way. The dutchman should be held in place with a waterproof glue such as resorcinol resin or epoxy.

Member Replacement. Replacement of individual members should be relatively straightforward. Often, the hardest part is removing the original piece without damaging the elements to remain. Once free, it can be used as a pattern for the new member, which should match the size and profile of the original. The new piece should be compatible with existing members in specie, cut, and grain direction. It should also have a moisture content similar to that of the surrounding wood. New members should be backprimed before installation to protect the concealed surfaces from water penetration. All sides, edges, and cut ends should be primed after the piece has been trimmed to fit. Wood replacement members should be installed using hot-dip galvanized or stainless steel fasteners.

Where entire existing elements on the façade are too deteriorated to be consolidated and patched or repaired with dutchmen, new replacement elements should be treated with an appropriate wood preservative after fabrication and before installation.

Major repair of concealed wood supports for projecting sheet metal elements is seldom undertaken. Deteriorated members are usually replaced with wood that has been treated with preservatives and fire retardants.

INSECT INFESTATIONS

Martin E. Weaver

Wood in service in buildings in the northeastern United States may be attacked by a surprisingly wide range of insect species including beetles, termites, and carpenter ants. Some people are surprised to discover that insect attacks are not limited to wood in rural buildings. For example, subterranean termites have been discovered actively attacking buildings in Central Park in New York City. The insects responsible for the damage usually are invisible. If the culprits cannot be seen the conservator can use the following evidence to identify them:

- The form of the frass or wood boredust, excreta and other debris that may be found in the tunnels or galleries;
- The diameter and form of the exit holes bored by the young adult insects as they emerge onto the surface of the wood; (normal diameters may vary from about 1/16 inch to 1/4 inch and the holes may be circular or elliptical);
- The form of the galleries or tunnels;
- The presence or absence of frass in the galleries or tunnels;
- Body parts or fragments of insects.

The most serious damage to timber is usually caused by species of insects in the three orders Coleoptera (beetles), Isoptera (termites), and Hymenoptera (ants and bees).

Beetles. Within the order of Coleoptera, a number of families are primarily responsible for damage to buildings in the northeastern United States. The Anobiidae family includes the common furniture beetle, the death watch beetle, and the drugstore beetle.

The frass is characteristically coarse and gritty, with bun-shaped or ellipsoidal pellets of compressed frass, which are loosely distributed through the galleries. Exit holes are circular and are about 1/8 inch or a little less in diameter. The damage is caused by larvae.

The Curculionidae or weevil family includes such species as Hexarthrum ulkeyi. Due to the prominent snoutlike projection on their heads, these beetles are also known as snouted beetles. They are normally found in wood that is also under attack by fungi and for this reason, are not usually regarded as a significant economic pest. Their emergence holes are circular, but may be slightly ragged in outline, and are very small, varying from less than 1/16 inch to 3/32 inch in diameter, easily identifying the attacker. Their frass is packed into galleries with some small ellipsoidal pellets. The damage is caused by larvae.

The Lyctidae or true powder post beetles include Lyctus brunneus (Steph.), the brown powder post beetle. These beetles prefer to attack maple, oak, birch, and other hardwoods. The frass is extremely fine and resembles flour. The circular emergence holes are small and regular and about 1/16 inch in diameter. The frass is loosely packed into the galleries, which run in all directions, often merging with one another. The damage is caused by larvae.

The Cerambycidae or "longhorn beetles" include Hylotrupes bajulus (L.), the Old House Borer. The frass is fairly fine and is loosely packed into the galleries, sometimes in short cylinders. The emergence holes are elliptical and may be as large as 1/4 inch x 3/8 inch. The damage is caused by larvae.

Termites. Within the order of Isoptera, the Eastern Subterranean Termite of the family Rhinotermitidae (species Reticulitermes flavipes Kollar), is one family of termites that attacks wood in service particularly in the northeastern United States. These termites live in excavated colonies below the ground surface and require a constant supply of moisture. The colonies consist mainly of egg-laying queens, soldiers, and workers. The workers build distinctive shelter tubes from soil and body fluids to protect their bodies against exposure to light and dehydration as they travel from the underground colony to the wood food source. The galleries, which are extensive and irregular, are readily distinguished by dark deposits of wet soil, excreta, and boredust. The damage is caused by the female worker caste. The interiors of wooden elements may be totally destroyed, leaving only a paper-thin external shell, which then collapses.

Carpenter Ants. Within the family of Hymenoptera, at least one family of ants is prominent in attacking wood in the northeastern United States: the species Camponotus pennsylvanicus (De Geer). The large, mainly black ants are approximately 1/2 inch long and are social insects, which usually but not exclusively establish their colonies consisting of queens, soldiers, workers, and drones in decayed or damp wood or in crevices between timbers. The wood is not eaten but is excavated to form the living chamber for the colony. The frass is ejected from the galleries to form large piles of coarse sawdust-like particles. The clean, frass-free gallery surfaces have a sandblasted appearance. The large adult ants may often be seen walking around in the area of the infested wood.

12

CAULKS AND SEALANTS

Deborah Slaton and Michael J. Sheffler

CAULKS AND SEALANTS are relatively elastic materials used to seal joints in building façades as part of the building's defense system against water penetration and air infiltration. Almost all walls have joints between the main surface material and the frames of doors and windows penetrating it. Other joints typically sealed include joints between large masses of masonry to allow for thermal expansion and contraction, joints between small sections of materials used to form larger ensembles (such as between sections of cast iron and pieces of sheet metal), and joints where roofing materials meet the rear surfaces of parapets. Sealants are especially critical in modern curtain wall structures, where they are used to weatherproof the joints between the glass panes and the mullions and muntins that support them.

HISTORY

Modern elastomeric sealants have only been available since the 1950s. Most historic buildings were built when the main types of caulking for joints were oil- and resin-based. The most common historic caulking material was a putty made with whiting and linseed oil. A paste made of white lead ground in linseed oil and turpentine was also used.

Some types of sealant commonly used in building applications in the past are not as widely used today; these include oil- and resin-based sealants mentioned and polysulfide sealants. Other sealants developed over the past several decades remain in common use, including silicone and polyurethane, both often used in high-rise construction, and acrylic, latex, and butyl-based sealants, more often used in smaller-scale construction and specialized applications.

EVALUATION AND ANALYSIS

Adhesion, cohesion, elasticity, and weatherability are the key characteristics of sealant used in assessing sealant performance. Failure of the sealant is usually related to one or more of these characteristics. Adhesion loss occurs between the sealant and the substrate. Signs of adhesion loss are separations along either side of the joint; but the separations may be difficult to perceive. Cohesion loss occurs within the sealant and is usually seen as separations within the body of the sealant. Generally, these separations occur parallel to the adjacent substrate. Elasticity loss is the loss of flexibility in the sealant and generally results in either adhesive or cohesive failure. Symptoms include the inability of the sealant to recover after deformation and increased hardness of the material. Degradation due to weathering is related to aging of the sealant. Typical indications of weathering include chalking, discoloration, cracking, wrinkling, erosion, or excessive softening.

Principal causes of sealant failure by the mechanisms described include the following:

Design Failures
Choice of inappropriate sealant for substrate or joint conditions.
Improper design of joint.
Lack of preconstruction testing.
Failure to specify proper application procedures.

Application Failures
Improper proportioning and mixing of sealant components.
Use of sealant near or beyond shelf life.
Inadequate substrate surface preparation.
Lack of appropriate sealant primer.
Poor environmental conditions during application and curing.

In-Service Failures
Physical or chemical damage.
Sealant has reached the end of its expected life.

Improper Sealant Selection

Certain sealants are appropriate for specific substrates, types of installations, or environments. The compatibility of the sealant with the substrate should also be evaluated prior to use. If the substrate is different on either side of the joint, the sealant must be compatible with both substrates, and different preparation may be required for each substrate.

Certain types of sealants cannot bond to certain other sealants. For example, most nonsilicone sealants will not develop a durable bond to silicone sealants. Also, some silicone sealants will not cure properly when installed over isobutylene sealants. Some sealants cannot bond to fluoropolymer finishes such as those used on architectural metals without the use of a primer and special preparation. In some instances, solvent-based sealant placed over certain paint coatings can soften or dissolve the coating.

Improper selection of a sealant for the required joint size can also contribute to sealant failure. For example, a sealant may not have the extension or compression capability to accommodate movement of the adjacent substrates. The expected movement of the substrate must be taken into account in designing the joint and in selecting a sealant with an appropriate modulus of elasticity and movement capability.

Many silicone sealants do not have good long-term adhesion if continuously wet or in standing water for extended periods. Performance testing should be done for wet conditions if the sealant will have to function in that capacity.

Improper Sealant Installation

Improper installation of sealant can lead to failure. Sealants are typically installed with compressible foam backer rod, polyethylene bond breaker tape, or other means to optimize sealant shape and to prevent three-sided adhesion (adherence of the sealant to the back as well as the sides of the joint). If these accessories are not properly installed, the sealant is likely to fail.

Installation during adverse environmental conditions will also result in problems. Sealant should not be installed during rainfall or very windy conditions. Wind-borne dirt and contaminants, such as found on dusty construction sites, can become embedded in uncured sealant. If sealant is installed when the substrate or ambient temperature is below 45 degrees Fahrenheit, the joint may be at its widest dimension through contraction of adjacent materials. The sealant may not be able to accommodate the subsequent expansion of the substrate and compression of the joint on heating. Conversely, if the sealant is installed when temperatures are above 90 degrees Fahrenheit, the joint may be at its narrowest dimension, and the sealant may be unable to accommodate expansion of the joint on cooling. At very cold temperatures, frost contamination on the surface can interfere with proper bonding and curing. At very hot temperatures, the sealant may flow. Sealant flow is especially likely to occur with dark-colored sealants in locations that are exposed to direct sunlight.

Sealants can fail if the substrate is improperly cleaned or primed, and can fail progressively if water gets behind an open-cell backer rod. Sealants can also fail if used beyond their shelf life. With silicones and urethanes, material that is out of date is usually characterized by a soft, tacky, and gummy consistency after curing.

Common problems with multicomponent urethanes are usually related to incomplete or improper mixing. If mixing is incomplete, portions of the sealant will be fluid or uncured. Incomplete curing can also be the result of using materials beyond their shelf life or using components from previously opened containers after contents have reacted with moisture.

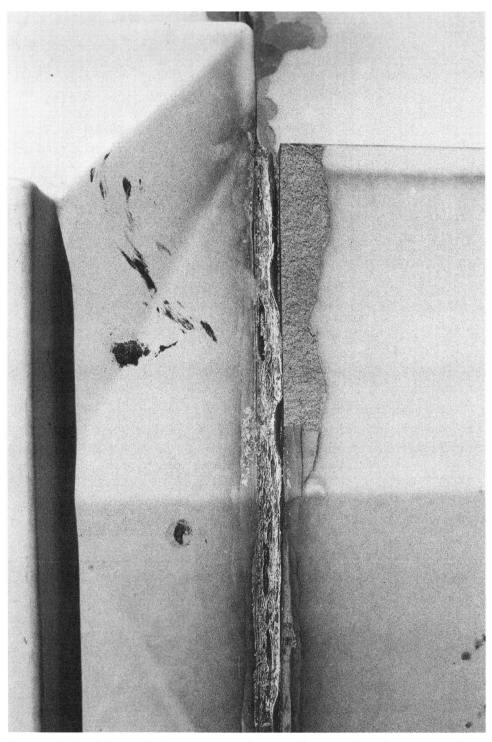

FIGURE 12.1. *Failure of sealants can occur because of improper installation, atmospheric conditions, or chemical attack.* James V. Banta, New York Landmarks Conservancy

Both cure and durability of sealants are affected by high temperatures. Sealant cured at high temperatures may become fluid and bubbled to a depth of 1/8 inch and gummy at lower levels. Curing at high temperatures (120 degrees Fahrenheit) can make some urethanes vulnerable to degradation in ultraviolet light, leading to severe reversion. Under ambient air temperatures of 80 to 90 degrees Fahrenheit, dark-colored substrates exposed to direct sunlight can reach temperatures exceeding 160 degrees Fahrenheit.

One-component sealants, such as some urethanes, cure by reacting with moisture in the air, in contrast to multicomponent urethanes, which cure by reaction of components. Some one-part urethanes are made with "moisture scavengers" such as calcium oxide, which serve to inhibit set until placement occurs. If particles of the scavenger are too large and are exposed on the surface, they will react with rainwater and can cause stains.

In-Service Failure

Even properly chosen and installed sealants can fail if they are physically damaged or attacked by chemicals during use. Although modern elastomeric sealants have longer expected life expectancies than those used in older buildings, even the best modern sealants will lose their resiliency as the end of their life span approaches. (Fig. 12.1)

Staining

Silicone sealants are susceptible to staining, either by dirt accumulation on the sealant itself (particularly under dirty environmental conditions) or by migration of the sealant plasticizer into the adjacent substrate. Stone substrates are particularly vulnerable to migration and staining from silicone sealants. Dirt accumulation on silicones, and on other sealants while they are still tacky, is a problem for small-scale construction where the wall surface is seen up close. Environmental dirt adheres to the sealant surface, adversely affecting sealant appearance. Accumulated dirt can be carried over the façade surface with rainwater runoff, causing unsightly staining. Staining can also occur where an elastomeric coating is applied over a caulked crack. Where light-colored sealants are applied over neoprene gaskets, the oil in the gasket may stain the sealants. Finally, improperly cured silicone sealants may leave deposits on glazing.

USING SEALANTS IN HISTORIC BUILDINGS

Sealants are in some ways unique elements of historic buildings: they are one of the few components likely to be replaced rather than conserved or restored. Ironically, in some older buildings, the existing sealant may itself be of historic interest. However, in many older and more recent historic buildings, the goal of the sealant repair project is to remove the existing sealant and to replace it with an inobtrusive, current sealant product that will provide good performance and durability. Increasing improvements in sealant technology have been made over the past 40 years, providing products with better overall performance. These improved sealants afford better protection for historic buildings as older sealants are replaced, even though the newer products may not match those originally used.

Although proper use of sealants in both working and nonworking joints will keep air, water, and other foreign elements out of a building, sealants are sometimes used inappropriately as quick fixes in attempts to keep water out of buildings with water leakage problems. This use may provide an effective short-term solution; however, unless all the factors affecting sealant selection and installation have been considered, the solution may not be a long-term one. In some cases, inappropriate use of sealant can cause additional damage. For example, joints or nonmoving cracks in masonry that should be repaired by pointing with mortar may be coated with sealant in an attempt to provide a quick solution. This approach may be detrimental to the entire building wall, since sealants can trap water within the wall. Also, sealants used to repair cracks in masonry materials tend to be visually obtrusive.

Sealant Selection

Proper sealant selection involves choosing the appropriate sealant for the conditions of the joints to be sealed. Factors involved in this selection include the substrates to which the sealant will be attached and how well the sealant will bond to them; whether the substrate is smooth or porous (and possibly susceptible to staining); the size and configuration of the joints to be sealed; whether the surface is horizontal, vertical, or sloped; anticipated joint movement; whether a specific color of sealant is required; whether painting of the sealant will be required; and the environmental conditions to which the building sealant will be subjected (including whether dirt accumulation is likely to occur). Table 12.1 includes a summary of performance characteristics and typical applications of the seven major types of sealants found on historic buildings or presently in common use.

Some sealant products are specifically designed to adhere to bituminous coatings. Careful analysis and identification of the bituminous coating is required to determine which sealant will be appropriate. Manufacturer's recommendations should be obtained for sealant selection, substrate preparation, and sealant application.

Where painting over sealant is required, such as when it is necessary for the appearance of the sealant to match that of the adjacent material, latex or acrylic sealants should be used, as they are readily paintable. (Even though some sealants today are termed siliconized, such as "siliconized latex," they essentially retain the characteristics of the base sealant, in this case latex.)

Table 12.1. SEALANTS
by Deborah Slaton and Michael J. Sheffler

Sealant Type	Physical Characteristics and Performance	Typical Uses	Advantages	Limitations
Oil and resin-based caulks	• Composed of calcium carbonate and drying oils such as linseed, fish, soybean, tung, and castor • Movement capability of +/- 2 percent to +/- 5 percent	• Bearing masonry joints experiencing little movement • Only building sealant type available until 1950s; widely used until that time; no longer typically used in building construction	• Paintable • Inexpensive • Easy to install	• Very limited movement capability, limited flexibility • Excessive shrinkage • Becomes excessively hard over time • Limited life expectancy (3 to 5 years; longer if regularly painted)
Polysulfide sealants	• Based on synthetic polysulfide polymer or rubber • Movement capability of +/- 25 percent • Considered a high-performance sealant	• High-rise masonry and curtain walls • Suitable for high-movement joints • Predominant sealant for high-rise use from 1950s through 1970s • Currently used in insulating glazing systems; tanks and pools; and some use in building façades	• Long history of use • Good movement capability • Low vapor transmission • High chemical resistance • Suitable for submerged applications • Can have more than 20 years service life	• Movement capability is more limited than some silicone and polyurethane sealants • Some products used through 1960s contained PCBs as plasticizer • Prior history of quality problems through 1970s
Silicone sealants	• Based on silicone polymer • Consist of high percentage of the silicone polymer; may contain fumed silica, calcium carbonate, ground quartz, carbon blacks, talcs, plasticizer, and other miscellaneous compounds • Movement capability of +100/- 50 percent • Considered a high-performance sealant	• High-rise metal and glass curtain walls • Insulating glazing systems and glazing systems • Structural glazing • Suitable for high-movement joints • Dates from early 1960s; currently predominant sealant in overall applications	• Long history of use • Excellent movement capability • Excellent adhesion to glass and metal surfaces • Excellent ultraviolet resistance • Color-stable • No shrinkage • Single component • Can have more than 20 years service life	• Tendency to stain porous substrates (such as stone, concrete, brick masonry) • Attracts dirt • Limited color range • Short tooling time • Some products have strong odor • Slightly more expensive than other comparable sealants

Table 12.1. continued

185

Table 12.1. SEALANTS *(continued)*

Sealant Type	Physical Characteristics and Performance	Typical Uses	Advantages	Limitations
Urethane sealants	• Based on polyurethane synthetic rubber • Composed of urethane polymer, urethane sealants usually include in their composition fillers, colorants, plasticizers, thixotropic agents, adhesion-promoting additives, and solvents • Movement capability of +/- 50 percent • Considered a high-performance sealant	• High-rise stone, concrete, and brick masonry façades • Paving systems • Suitable for high-movement joints • Dates from mid-1960s; currently extensively used in high-rise construction	• Long history of use • Excellent movement capability • Good adhesion to porous surfaces • Good ultraviolet resistance • Good abrasion resistance • Long working time for multicomponent • Negligible shrinkage • Good for wider joints (greater than 1 inch) • Can have more than 20 years service life	• Requires mixing of multiple components at time of application to achieve high-movement capabilities; successful application depends on proper mixing and skill of applicator • Poor water-immersion resistance • Single component requires long cure time
Acrylic sealants	• Based on acrylic polymer • Include fillers such as calcium carbonate with silica, and solvents such as xylol, catalysts, thixotropic agents and plasticizers • Movement capability of not more than +/- 12.5 percent	• Small-scale construction • Peak usage in mid-1970s	• Paintable • Easy cleanup after application • Single component • Inexpensive	• Limited movement capability • Poor movement capability at low temperatures • Long cure time
Latex sealants	• Based on acrylic, styrene-acrylic, vinyl acrylic, polyvinyl acetate, or styrene butalene • Components include water, ground calcium carbonate, plasticizers, small amounts of mineral spirits, ethylene glycol, surfactants, and pigments • Movement capability of not more than +/- 7.5 percent	• Small-scale construction • Used since 1960s	• Paintable • Easy cleanup after application • Single component • Inexpensive • Good adhesion without priming	• Limited movement capability • Breaks down in constant wet condition • Becomes hard with curing • Some products require long cure time

Table 12.1. continued

Table 12.1. SEALANTS *(continued)*

Sealant Type	Physical Characteristics and Performance	Typical Uses	Advantages	Limitations
Butyl sealants	• Based on synthetic rubber • Components include talc powder, calcium carbonate filler, polybutylene, mineral spirits, adhesion promoters, and other compounds • Movement capability of up to +/- 7.5 percent	• Glazing joints and splice seals in window units • Synthetic rubber replacement for natural rubber in World War II; sealants used since mid-1950s	• Low vapor transmission • Single component • Good for specialized use in window systems • Good life expectancy	• Limited movement capability • Not suitable for exposed joint applications • Very long cure time • High shrinkage

Preparation of the Joint

Proper joint preparation is critical to successful sealant performance. Substrate preparation requires that the joint surfaces be cleaned of dust, dirt, oils, greases, previous caulks and sealants, and all other substances that might adversely affect the bond between the sealant and the substrate. Joint cleaning should follow the manufacturer's directions for the sealant and substrate.

Where a joint has been previously sealed with a sealant—whether of the same type as the sealant to be installed or of a different type—the surfaces of the joint must be cleaned by mechanical means, using a knife or grinder, or by chemical means, using a solvent such as isopropyl alcohol. If mechanical means are used, care must be taken to avoid scratching the adjacent substrate. If chemicals are used, they should first be tested to assure that they will not adversely affect the substrate by staining, removing paint coatings, or otherwise damaging the surface. Any surface to receive sealant must be free of dust and contaminants and must be dry.

It is desirable to completely remove existing sealant. If removal is not possible, and sealing to the existing residue is desired, the residue should be examined for adhesion. The ability of the new sealant to adhere will be dependent on the bond of the existing sealant. When existing sealant is replaced, it should be removed carefully and disposed of properly to prevent staining of adjacent building materials. Also, as noted in Table 12.1, some older sealants may contain materials that require special disposal.

Sealant may be applied over a painted surface, provided that the paint coating is solidly adhered to the substrate and is in sound and clean condition, free of peeling or chalking. The coating in the joint must be properly prepared to receive the sealant as described.

Priming

Primers are sometimes required to condition joint surfaces to provide maximum sealant bond. Priming is usually not required with acrylic and latex sealants because these products have sufficient adhesion for small-scale construction, provided the substrate has been properly prepared. For silicones and urethanes, application of a primer recommended by the sealant manufacturer is often required.

Sealant Profile

In addition to preparation of the substrate, another key to proper installation is creating the correct sealant profile. To achieve a proper sealant profile, the sealant depth must be controlled during installation. Generally, although it varies among different sealant types and products, the depth of the sealant should be approximately half the width of the joint. For very narrow joints (approximately 1/4 inch or less in width),

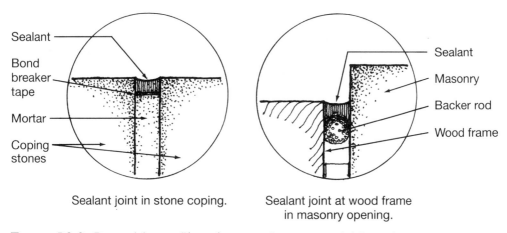

Sealant
Bond breaker tape
Mortar
Coping stones

Sealant
Masonry
Backer rod
Wood frame

Sealant joint in stone coping.

Sealant joint at wood frame
in masonry opening.

FIGURE 12.2. *Proper joint profile and preparation are essential for optimum sealant performance. A backer rod is used to control depth of sealant. Backer rods and bond breaker tapes prevent sealant from bonding to surfaces other than the sides of the joint.*

however, the depth should usually match the joint width. Depth is usually controlled using backer rod. (Fig. 12.2)

After the existing sealant is removed and the joint surface prepared, backer rod is placed in the joint. Backer rod is formed of a compressible polyurethane or polyethylene foam formed in a cylindrical shape. The size of the backer rod selected should be slightly wider than the joint width so that it will maintain its position after being placed in the joint. In certain situations, particularly where existing sealant is difficult or impossible to remove, bond breaker tape consisting of polyethylene formed in strips of varying widths is installed along the joint to prevent the new sealant from bonding to the existing sealant. In addition to providing proper joint profile, backer rod and bond breaker tape prevent the sealant from bonding to other than the sides of the joint. Sealant that is bonded only to the sides of the joint will accommodate sealant movement properly. Generally, the sealant should bond to a depth of 1/4 inch width of substrate on either side of the joint; however, this dimension varies with different manufacturers.

Sealant Application

Before applying the sealant, it may be desirable to protect the surfaces on either side of the joint with nonresidue tape or other appropriate protection if there is a chance that sealant might accidently be applied to them. The sealant should be applied following manufacturer's directions for environmental conditions and application procedures. In the case of two-component products, proper proportioning and mixing is essential.

Unless an existing aesthetic sealant feature is to be matched, the sealant should be tooled to a concave profile. This profile allows the sealant to most effectively accommodate joint movement. Tooling should be performed with a dry metal trowel that matches the joint width, and care should be taken to avoid scratching adjacent surfaces. During tooling, the sealant should be compressed against the backer rod and bond breaker tape to eliminate air pockets and ensure proper contact with the substrate.

Curing

Special precautions are usually not required for curing of sealants. However, consideration should be given to installing sealants during moderate temperatures. Manufacturer's product literature provides guidance on the range of temperatures at which sealants should be installed. High temperatures will make the sealant more viscous, and low temperatures will make the sealant stiffer. In both cases, installation will be more difficult. Also, if sealants are installed during moderate and fairly steady temperatures, the amount of movement experienced during curing will be minimized.

Budget constraints frequently affect the selection of products and methods of installation for historic buildings and small-scale construction. Where sealants are concerned, however, it is well worth taking the time to select the most appropriate sealant and spending more money to achieve better performance. Because labor costs for the installation of sealants typically constitute more than three-fourths of the cost of a sealant replacement project, the material costs are relatively low. A small incremental increase in the cost of the materials that would not significantly affect the budget may significantly improve long-term performance and durability.

SELECTED
BIBLIOGRAPHY

Amoroso, G. G., and Fassina, V. *Stone Decay and Conservation*. Amsterdam: Elsevier, 1983.

Ashurst, John and Nicola. *Practical Building Conservation*, Vol. 1-5. New York: Halstead Press, a division of John Wiley & Sons, Inc., 1988.

Clifton, James R. *Cleaning Stone and Masonry*. Philadelphia: American Society for Testing and Materials, 1986.

Condit, Carl W. *American Building: Materials and Techniques from the First Colonial Settlements to the Present*. Chicago: University of Chicago Press, 1968.

Coney, William B. *Preservation of Historic Concrete: Problems and General Approaches; Preservation Brief 15*. Washington, DC: U.S. Department of the Interior.

Cowden, Adrienne B., and Wessel, David P. "Cast Stone." In *Twentieth-Century Building Materials*, edited by Thomas C. Jester. New York: McGraw-Hill, 1995.

Elliott, Cecil D. *The Development of Materials and Systems for Buildings*. Cambridge, MA.: The MIT Press, 1994.

Gayle, Margot, Look, David W., and Waite, John G. *Metals in America's Historic Buildings*. Washington, DC: U.S. Department of the Interior, 1992.

Grimmer, Anne E. *Keeping It Clean: Removing Exterior Dirt, Paint, Stains and Graffiti from Historic Masonry Buildings*. Washington, DC: Preservation Assistance Division, National Park Service, U.S. Department of the Interior, 1988.

——*Dangers of Abrasive Cleaning to Historic Buildings; Preservation Brief 6*. Washington, D.C.: Technical Preservation Services Division, Heritage Conservation and Recreation Service, U.S. Department of the Interior, 1979.

Historical Trades Corporation. *Clem Labine's Traditional Building*. Brooklyn, NY.

Bimonthly periodical providing information and sources of products for the restoration of historic buildings.

Hoadley, R. Bruce. *Understanding Wood*. Newtown, CT: The Taunton Press, Inc., 1980.

Hornbostel, Caleb. *Construction Materials: Types, Uses and Applications, 2nd ed.* New York: John Wiley & Sons, Inc., 1991.

Jandl, H. Ward. *The Technology of Historic American Buildings: Studies of the Materials, Craft Processes, and the Mechanization of Building Construction.* Washington, DC: The Foundation for Preservation Technology, 1983.

Jester, Thomas C., ed. *Twentieth-Century Building Materials*. New York: McGraw-Hill, 1995.

Lynch, Michael F., and Higgins, William J. *The Maintenance and Repair of Architectural Sandstone.* New York: New York Landmarks Conservancy, 1982.

Mack, Robert C. "The Manufacture and Use of Architectural Terra Cotta in the United States." In *The Technology of Historic American Buildings: Studies of the Materials, Craft Processes, and the Mechanization of Building Construction*, edited by H. Ward Jandl. Washington, DC: Foundation for the Association for Preservation Technology, 1983.

——*Repointing Mortar Joints in Historic Brick Buildings; Preservation Brief 2.* Washington, D.C.: Technical Preservation Services Division, Heritage Conservation and Recreation Service, U.S. Department of the Interior, 1980.

McKee, Harley J. *Introduction to Early American Masonry.* Washington, DC: National Trust for Historic Preservation and Columbia University, 1973.

Moss, Roger. *Paint in America: The Colors of Historic Buildings.* Washington, DC: The Preservation Press, 1994.

New York Landmarks Conservancy. *Repairing Old and Historic Windows: A Manual for Architects and Homeowners.* Washington, DC: The Preservation Press, 1992.

Panek, Julian R., and Cook, John, P. *Construction Sealants and Adhesives.* New York: John Wiley & Sons, Inc., 1991.

Park, Sharon C. *The Use of Substitute Materials on Historic Building Exteriors; Preservation Brief 16.* Washington, DC: Preservation Assistance Division, National Park Service, U.S. Department of the Interior.

Price, C.A. *Stone Conservation: An Overview of Current Research.* Santa Monica: The Getty Conservation Institute, 1996.

Ramsey/Sleeper. *Traditional Details: For Building Restoration, Renovation, and Rehabilitation from the 1932-1951 Editions of Architectural Graphic Standards.* New York: John Wiley & Sons, Inc., 1991.

Revere Copper and Brass, Inc. *Copper and Common Sense.* New York: Revere Copper and Brass, Inc., 1982.

Schaffer, R. J. *The Weathering of Natural Building Stones.* London: HMSO, 1932, reprinted 1972.

Scheffler, Michael J., and Connolly, James D. "Building Sealants." In *Twentieth-Century Building Materials*, edited by Thomas C. Jester. New York: McGraw-Hill, 1995.

Slaton, Deborah, and Hunderman, Harry J. "Terra Cotta." In *Twentieth-Century Building Materials*, edited by Thomas C. Jester. New York: McGraw-Hill, 1995.

SMACNA. *Architectural Sheet Metal Manual*, 5th ed. Chantilly, VA: SMACNA, 1993.

Suprenant, Bruce A., and Schuller, Michael P. *Nondestructive Evaluation & Testing of Masonry Structures*. Addison, IL: The Aberdeen Group, 1994.

Tiller, de Teel Patterson. *The Preservation of Historic Glazed Architectural Terra-Cotta; Preservation Brief 7*. Washington, DC: Preservation Assistance Division, National Park Service, U.S. Department of the Interior, 1979.

Waite, John G. *The Maintenance and Repair of Architectural Cast Iron: A Technical Preservation Brief*. New York: New York Landmarks Conservancy, 1991.

Weaver, Martin E., and Matero, F. G. *Conserving Buildings: Guide to Techniques and Materials*. New York: John Wiley & Sons, Inc., 1993.

Weaver, Martin E. *Removing Graffiti from Masonry: A Technical Preservation Brief*. New York: New York Landmarks Conservancy, 1995.

Weeks, Kay D., and Look, David W. *Exterior Paint Problems on Historic Woodwork; Preservation Brief 10*. Washington, DC: Preservation Assistance Division, National Park Service, U.S. Department of the Interior, 1982.

Winkler, Erhard M. *Stone in Architecture: Properties, Durability*. New York: Springer-Verlag, 1994.

Zahner, L. William. *Architectural Metals: A Guide to Selection, Specification, and Performance*. New York: John Wiley & Sons, Inc., 1995.

INDEX